Have You Met Me Yet?

A Story of Survival

By

Troy Hamilton

Published by:

Dedication

For my Mum, the one that has loved me all of my life. And to my daughter, the one that I will love for the rest of mine.

Acknowledgement

To my donor family. Simply...THANK YOU!

Letter to My Donor Family

On the 26th of June, 2018, I was extremely lucky to receive the amazingly beautiful gift of a life-saving kidney. There are no words that I could possibly say that could convey my gratitude, except to say that I am absolutely humbled by this gift.

I was first diagnosed on the 13th of June, 2016.

Since that day, I have put every ounce of effort and force of will into this body. Firstly, to prepare it for the day that I hoped would come (in the way of a kidney donation). And then to preserve this body with its new kidney to the absolute best of my ability.

There are no days off for me. I work hard on this body every single day. It's the only way I know how to respect my donor and his family.

This incredible gift has allowed me to see my daughter not only graduate from high school, but also graduate from university with a Bachelor of Arts. My daughter has been with me through this since she was twelve years old. I got her involved and had her check my work, just to make sure everything was good. It was a way to normalise it for her. And she's been a real trooper for me. She now lives a wonderful life with her partner, and I am so proud to be a part of her life. I especially love being able to do 'Dad' type jobs for her. It makes me feel worthwhile and valued. This would not have been possible without your wonderful gift. I just wish I had the words.........

I am sorry that I haven't reached out before, but I was concerned that I could never measure up to the one that you lost. I was worried that you might think me unworthy, or too old, or just not the right person to receive this gift.

That has just fuelled me even more to prove that I am deserving by putting in all the work that I do. All my health professionals tell me that I'm doing too much, but it could never be too much. For me, it's about respect. And I show my respect by doing the work.

Unfortunately, for all of that to happen, you had to lose someone who was so very, very precious to you.

I am so, so sorry that happened to you, and I give you my word to wake up every day and to try to be the best possible version of me that I can be.

With heartfelt sorrow and thanks.

My donor saved not only my life, but many, many others.

On behalf of myself and those others.

THANK YOU!

Table of Contents

Chapter 1:
Defiance

Have You Met Me Yet?

Eight years ago, on the thirteenth of June,
A white room closed around me like a fist,
Somewhere between the beeping and the bloom,
Of faces leaning in to read what I'd missed.

"Hey, Troy, don't you know that you're going to die?"
"In fact, we're all amazed that you're still alive,"
"You see, you're down to just 1% of kidney functionality,"
"Hey, Troy, are you okay? Are you finding it hard to breathe?"

"Nah, Mate, I'm alright, I've got lots of fight left,"
"You tell me that I'm dying, but have you met me yet?"
"You see there's something about me, that you don't know,"
"I've been a fighter from birth, I can take the blows."

I went to a doctor, for a simple health check,
"Hey, Troy, while you're here, let's do some blood tests,"
"Are your kidneys okay? Are they working alright?"
"As far as I'm aware, doctor, my kidneys are doing fine,"
"Okay then, take these pills, your blood pressure's kinda high,"
"We should have all your results, on Wednesday around five."

"Oh, it seems, I may have prescribed you, some of the wrong meds,"
"Your kidneys are now dying, in fact they're almost dead,"
"You need to go to the hospital, there's not much time left,"
But I couldn't go, I had my daughter, it was our weekend.

"Hey, Troy, don't you know that you're going to die?"
"In fact, we're all amazed that you're still alive,"
"You see, you're down to just 1% of kidney functionality,"
"Hey, Troy, are you okay? Are you finding it hard to breathe?"

"Nah, Mate, I'm alright, I've got lots of fight left,"
"You tell me that I'm dying, but have you met me yet?"
"You see there's something about me, that you don't know,"
"I've been a fighter from birth, I can take the blows."

We've got a drug for this, a drug for that, and everything in between,
Here you go, just swallow them down, and then take some more at three.

Now I'm medicated, and everything feels so slow,
Before I was asymptomatic, but now I'm in the throes,
I've mastered the old man shuffle, just one foot in front of the next,
If I was going any slower, I'd be going in reverse instead.

"Hey, Troy, are you okay? Are you finding it hard to breathe?"
"If you are, we can help you, we've got all the pills you need,"
"Well, we don't want to worry you, but we've just got your results,"
"And we're very sad to say, that we really don't like your odds,"

"Well, call me a fool to believe in myself, I don't need your fucking help,"
"Here you are casting your shadows of doubt, but I will never doubt myself,"
"You don't even know me, I've got lots of fight left,"
"You tell me that I'm dying, but have you met me yet?"

We've got a drug for this, a drug for that, and everything in between,
Here you go, just swallow them down, and then take some more at three.

"Prepare for constipation, loss of urination, and constant irritation,"
"There's going to be frustration, risk of inflammation, as your system breaks down,"
"Immunosuppression, risk of rejection, it's just how it's all turned out,"
"But we're here to listen, if you wish it, until your last breath falls out."

It's a dance between two strangers, and neither of us chose,
This partner or this music or this body on the floor,
It drags me through its tempo and I step upon its toes,
But I refuse to waltz my way right out the door.

We've got a drug for this, a drug for that, and everything in between,
Here you go, just swallow them down, and then take some more at three.

Now the drugs aren't working anymore, and I'm dressed all in purple,
They're cutting me open again today, we're just waiting for the surgeons,
Unfortunately, it's not a one off thing, I've lost count of all my procedures,
But I will tell you one thing I know, I won't be attending my own funeral.

Counting all the doctors, 1, 2, 3, standing around a hospital room, all looking at me,
"We've got your new results, and they're not pretty, creatinine is high, eGFR is dipping,"
"We've got you on the transplant list, cross your fingers and hope for the best,"
"It might be time to finalise things, write a will, and all the rest."

"Hey, Troy, don't you know that you're going to die?"
"In fact, we're all amazed that you're still alive,"
"You see, you're down to just 1% of kidney functionality,"
"Hey, Troy, are you okay? Are you finding it hard to breathe?"

"Nah, Mate, I'm alright, I've got lots of fight left,"
"You tell me that I'm dying, but have you met me yet?"
"You see there's something about me, that you don't know,"
"I've been a fighter from birth, I can take the blows."

It was Six years ago, on the twenty sixth day of June,
I was in the shower that morning, my phone wasn't in the room,
I didn't hear the phone ring, I didn't see the missed call,
5 minutes later, there was a banging at my front door,
It was my brother, he said, "they've got a kidney for you!"
I had to get to the city, and I had to get there soon.

As I'm sure you can guess, I've made it to today,
But it hasn't been easy, I've had to sculpt a new me,
I've had to make changes, and I've made my mistakes,
But at least I'm alive today, so that I can make them again.

"Hey, Troy, don't you know that you're going to die?"
"In fact, we're all amazed that you're still alive,"
"You see, you're down to just 1% of kidney functionality,"
"Hey, Troy, are you okay? Are you finding it hard to breathe?"

"You tell me that I'm dying, but I've got lots of fight left,"
"After all, how would you know, have you met me yet?"

11 August, 2024

Nail Gun

"So, tell me, Troy. Do you have a support network?
"Well, to tell you the truth, I kinda just do for myself,"
"What do you mean, Troy? Who do you call when you hurt?"
"Well, I've reached out before, but everyone was out,"
"So, explain it to me, Troy. You're doing this all alone?"
"Sure, I just do what I need, I can do this on my own,"
"C'mon now, Troy, you know you're dying, why not just relent?"
"I've just got five words for you, have you met me yet?"

It was in the year of 2016, on the day of June Thirteen,
Yeah, you've heard it before, you know what I mean,
That's when I got that call, "Troy, you've got renal disease,"
That's when my world changed...but I wouldn't let it beat me.

So, it came to the time to biopsy my kidney, and it sure as Hell wasn't fun,
A nurse held my hand, while it felt like being shot with a nail gun,
I kept my mouth shut, I had to prove to myself that I'm strong,
I don't believe in luck, I knew I had to do this on my own.

"You've got a pill for this, another one for that, and everything in between,"
"But what you can't give me, is a pill, that will cure me of this disease."

"So, tell me, Troy. Do you have a support network?
"Well, to tell you the truth, I kinda just do for myself,"
"What do you mean, Troy? Who do you call when you hurt?"
"Well, I've reached out before, but everyone was out,"
"So, explain it to me, Troy. You're doing this all alone?"
"Sure, I just do what I need, I can do this on my own,"
"C'mon now, Troy, you know you're dying, why not just relent?"
"I've just got five words for you, have you met me yet?"

"Hey, Troy. Are you okay? Are you finding it hard to breathe?"
"Nah, Mate. I'm alright, you don't need to worry about me,"
"But, tell us how you really feel, I am sure that we can help,"
"What? Like in a practical sense? You can feed me, clean me, and give me a house?"
"We can't exactly do all of that, it's really not within our means,"
"So, what you're really saying, is that I can only rely on me?"

"You've got a pill for this, another one for that, and everything in between,"
"But what you can't give me, is a pill, that will cure me of this disease."

Yeah, I know it sounds relentless, every chapter full of fight,
But relentless is the only tempo that has kept me in the light,
But in this life, it's a fight that no one else can see,
A slow war waged in silence, in the blood and the marrow of me,
It's not about good versus evil, or right versing wrong,
It's about rising above, and surviving against the odds.

"Hey, Troy. Are you okay? Are you finding it hard to breathe?"
"To tell you the truth, you're in my face and you're kinda suffocating me,"
"You've got to give me space, and let me do things my own way,"
"'Cause when it comes down to it, it's me I'm trying to save."

"You tell me that I'm dying, but I've got lots of fight left,"
"You might be diagnosing, but have you met me yet?"

"You've got a pill for this, another one for that, and everything in between"
"But what you can't give me, is a pill, that will cure me of this disease"

"So, tell me, Troy. Do you have a support network?
"Well, to tell you the truth, I kinda just do for myself,"
"What do you mean, Troy? Who do you call when you hurt?"
"Well, I've reached out before, but everyone was out,"
"So, explain it to me, Troy. You're doing this all alone?"
"Sure, I just do what I need, I can do this on my own,"
"C'mon now, Troy, you know you're dying, why not just relent?"
"I've just got five words for you, have you met me yet?"

"Sure, I can do this, I can do this on my own,"
"But I've got to be thankful, for the nurse that held my hand,"
"She didn't have to do it, no, not at all,"
"While it just felt like, I was being shot by a nail gun."

"Hey, Troy. Are you okay? Are you finding it hard to breathe?"
"Nah, Mate, I've got lots of fight, lots of fight left in me."

15 August, 2024

Into the Noise

Sometimes I need to put myself right into the noise,
Just so I can hear my own Goddamn voice,
Make it all mean nothing, no time to overthink,
Give myself a break, fuck it, have another drink,
The traffic, the sirens, the people fighting right next door.

The static, the lying, the crying baby on the floor,
Needles stuck to the carpet, from the night before,
Shitty nappies on the table, as the police knock on the door.

Welcome to my Hell, it has its own personal pleasures,
As if you couldn't tell, it involves whips and leather,
I'm not really sure what they are doing up the street,
But it seems to be a place where men like to meet.

There's a red light burning 42, bleeding through the door,
A woman's voice cuts the dark like something split and raw,
The silence after, worse than anything said before,
It seeps beneath my floorboards, settles in the floor.

How can I put myself right into the noise,
How can I find a way to just ignore,
The breaking of the windows, the slamming of the doors,
Fuck, I really need to put myself right into the noise,
Before something happens... that requires force,
Before something happens........that requires remorse.
Before something happens........

How can I help myself when everyone else is at war,
How do I get to choose myself when I can see blood on the floor,
How do I get to live my life when this world is all about war,
How can I believe in myself when my body is broken and worn,
But that is why I have to put myself...right into the fucking noise.

That is how I revive myself, that is how I am reborn,
Into a new version of myself, scraped clean, reborn,
I am not afraid of this world; you're the one who's less sure,
You never walked in my shoes, yet somehow you were worn,
By the weight of a life you only watched from the shore,
Don't you remember the footsteps you took....as you walked on out.

Where are my choices? Maybe buried in the noise,
Somewhere beneath the sirens and the shattered broken glass,
Or locked inside a version of myself who was a boy,
Before this life pressed down and made the future into past.

I know nobody knows how I feel right now,
And that's all right, I've got my big boy pants on now,
I have fallen before, but here I now stand proud,
But, fuck, this life is really messing with me right now,
No one really knows, and that's okay somehow.

I really need to lose the noise,
It's kinda fucking with my mind,
Can you just whisper with your voice?
And I will return in kind...

Except, everything's crazy right now,
I just can't find my feet on the ground,
This life has turned upside down,
And there's nothing.......to land on right now.

How can I help myself when everyone else is at war,
How do I get to choose myself, when all I can see is blood on the floor,
How do I get to live my life when this world is all about war,
How can I believe in myself when my body is broken and worn,
But that is why I have to put myself.............right into the fucking noise.

How can I put myself right into the noise,
How can I find a way to just ignore,
The breaking of the windows, the slamming of the doors,
Fuck, I really need to put myself right into the noise,
Before something happens... that requires force,
Before something happens...that requires remorse,
Before something happens...

Before something happens...
...I really need to put myself into the noise.

3 March, 2026

Chapter 2:
Not My Time

Kill My Weak

Now we fast forward, to year of twenty twenty four,
And now I have to work harder, than I ever have before,
You see, something happened, that I wasn't ready for,
I've had battles on several fronts, and now I have to go to war.

"Hey, Troy. Are you okay? Are you finding it hard to breathe?"
"Your numbers are now falling again, in fact, the curve is steep,"
"At this point, it's only indicatory, but we're sure you know what it means,"
"It looks like your IgA has returned, it's a return of your kidney disease."

"Fuck this shit, I'm sick of it, you keep on saying that I'm dying,"
"I'm tougher than this, and I'll prove it, I'll never give up trying,"
"You just think, I can't do this, but just wait, and you'll see me flying,"
"I don't quit, I'm stronger than this, you'll never see me crying,"
"I might have been, on my knees, but I knew I that this wasn't my end,"
"'Cause the blood I bleed, feed through machines, dialysis was just another step,"
"But I know me, I'll kill my weak, I will always fight until my last breath,"
"Because after all, you might be diagnosing me, but have you met me yet?"

"You've got pills for this, a drug for that, something to cover all needs,"
"But what you can't give me, is the only thing I need, a cure for this bloody disease."

"We understand there's also housing issues, do you have somewhere to sleep?"
"We can write a support letter for you, but of course, there's no guarantees,"
"We'd really love to help you, but there are so many others in need,"
"There's only so much to go around, maybe you could come back next week?"

"Yeah, that's okay, I understand, I never was one for holding out my hand,"
"Make no mistake, I only ask once, and then you'll never hear me asking again."

"You've got pill for this, a drug for that, something to cover all needs,"
"But what you can't give me, is the only thing I need, a cure for this bloody disease."

"Fuck this shit, I'm sick of it, you keep on saying that I'm dying,"
"I'm tougher than this, and I'll prove it, I'll never give up trying,"
"You just think, I can't do this, but just wait and you'll see me flying,"
"I don't quit, I'm stronger than this, you'll never see me crying,"
"I might have been, on my knees, but I knew I that this wasn't my end,"
"'Cause the blood I bleed, feed through machines, dialysis was just another step,"
"But I know me, I'll kill my weak, I will always fight until my last breath,"
"Because after all, you might be diagnosing me, but have you met me yet?"

Now here we are, in the year of twenty twenty four,
And now I have to work harder, than I ever have before.

"Hey, Troy. Are you okay? Are you finding it hard to breathe?"
"I'm doing the very best that I can, to be a better me"
"What exactly do you mean by that? Do you have a routine?"
"Sure, I do. It's a simple one, to be my strength and kill my weak."

Now I'm working even harder, than I ever have before,
Lifting my 10kg dumbbells, watching the sweat fall on the floor,
I've got my walking shoes on, as I'm heading out the door,
Building myself back up again, yeah, I'm ready for this war.

"You've got pill for this, a drug for that, something to cover all needs,"
"But what you can't give me, is the only thing I need, a cure for this bloody disease."

"Hey, Troy. Are you okay? Are you finding it hard to breathe?"
"Nah, Mate. I'm alright, I'm stronger than this disease,"
"C'mon, Troy. It's perfectly normal to admit that you're scared and weak,"
"Why do you want to bring me down? Instead of believing in me?"

"You've got pill for this, a drug for that, something to cover all needs,"
"But what you can't give me is the only thing I need, a cure for this bloody disease."

"Fuck this shit, I'm sick of it, you keep on saying that I'm dying,"
"I'm tougher than this, and I'll prove it, I'll never give up trying,"
"You just think, I can't do this, but just wait and you'll see me flying,"
"I don't quit, I'm stronger than this, you'll never see me crying,"
"I might have been, on my knees, but I knew I that this wasn't my end,"
"'Cause the blood I bleed, feed through machines, dialysis was just another step,"
"But I know me, I'll kill my weak, I will always fight until my last breath,"
"Because after all, you might be diagnosing me, but have you met me yet?"

24 September, 2024

Work

I've gotta work, I've gotta work, I've gotta work, work, work,
There's a chant in my head, that says if you don't wanna be dead,
I've gotta work, I've gotta work, I've gotta work, work, work,
There's a chant in my head, that says that I never can relent,
I've gotta work, I've gotta work, I've gotta work, work, work.

We're still in the year of twenty twenty four,
And I've got another procedure tomorrow, that I'm not looking towards,
I know it's a simple one, but I have my reservations just the same,
It's much later in the week, I need to know that my surgeon is on the game.

"Hey, Man. Are you the one that's cutting me open today?"
"I need to know that you are focused, today's not a day for mistakes,"
"You see, I've had to work my arse off, just to be alive today,"
"So, make sure you don't fuck it up, or I'll haunt you from beyond my grave,"
"I'm only joking, I'm just kidding, I know you won't make that mistake,"
"I'll promise not to die on the table, as long as you don't kill me today."

"You can rest assured, Troy. We've got all the angles covered,"
"It's just a simple procedure, we know that you'll recover,"
"But, just in case there's a problem, do we have your updated emergency contact?"
"We just have to cross the t's and dot the i's, it's just the legal procedure."

"Yeah, Mate. All my info is current, that sounds like an admin thing, I just want to keep living,"
"You guys are the biggest dealers in the world, how about we don't make it about money,"
"You could be doing better things, instead of just worrying about the budget,"
"How about you remember humanity, you could ease so much suffering,"
"I know that it's all an insurance thing, how about offering some comfort."

And because I can't trust those, that claim to try to save me,
I have to be the hero in my story, I have to be Hercules,
And now I have to....

I've gotta work, I've gotta work, I've gotta work, work, work,
There's a chant in my head, that says if you don't wanna be dead,
I've gotta work, I've gotta work, I've gotta work, work, work,
There's a chant in my head, that says that I never can relent,
I've gotta work, I've gotta work, I've gotta work, work, work.

"Hey, Man. Are you the one that's cutting me open today?"
"I need to know that you are focused, today's not a day for mistakes,"
"You see, I've had to work my arse off, just to be alive today,"
"So, make sure you don't fuck it up, or I'll haunt you from beyond my grave,"
"I'm only joking, I'm just kidding, I know you won't make that mistake,"
"I'll promise not to die on the table, as long as you don't kill me today."

I've gotta work, I've gotta work, I've gotta work, work, work,,
There's a chant in my head, that says if you don't wanna be dead,
I've gotta work, I've gotta work, I've gotta work, work, work,
There's a chant in my head, that says that I never can relent,
I've gotta work, I've gotta work, I've gotta work, work, work,
I guess I better finish this up, I still have some prep to do,
I've done this before, so to me, it's really nothing new,

I'm gonna take my pills tonight, and raise them to the dark,
Because tomorrow's not a promise, but the fight is in my heart.

25 September, 2024

Crystal Ballin'

Now we are fast forwarding, to the year of twenty twenty five,
Yeah, I'm crystal ballin', but it's the year that I'm going to thrive,
I'm going to keep my feet on the ground, but you'll still see me fly,
Yeah, I'm crystal ballin', but it's time to celebrate this life,
I've been on my knees before, but I always knew I would rise once more,
Yeah, I'm crystal ballin', but I know I'm stronger than before,
It's time for something more, something to strive towards,
Yeah, I'm crystal ballin', you just wait and you'll see me soar.

"Hey, Troy. Are you okay? Are you finding it hard to breathe?"
"I'm kinda sick of you asking me that, just take a look at me!"
"I am so much stronger than you think, why can't you just believe?"
"I guess I'll just prove myself again, 'cause the only one I can rely on is me."

"No, listen, Troy. We only have your best interests at heart,"
"No, you listen, You don't know, with your numbers and your charts,"
"I've always been a survivor, you just watch me beat the odds,"
"I've done it before and I'll do it again, 2025, here I come!"

"You keep trying to slow me down, don't you know that I know by now?"
"You've got a pill for this and another for that, don't you know I've worked it out?"
"I'm not a fool, I'm not a sheep, I know my choices and my consequences meet,"
"You must have mistaken me for someone else... I am not one of the meek."

Now we are fast forwarding, to the year of twenty twenty five,
Yeah, I'm crystal ballin', but it's the year that I'm going to thrive,
I'm going to keep my feet on the ground, but you'll still see me fly,
Yeah, I'm crystal ballin', but it's time to celebrate this life,
I've been on my knees before, but I always knew I would rise once more,
Yeah, I'm crystal ballin', but I know I'm stronger than before,
It's time for something more, something to strive towards,
Yeah, I'm crystal ballin', you just wait and you'll see me soar.

I'm gonna celebrate this life, with every living breath that I have left,
I'll live in all the highs, thank God that I'm alive, 'cause it's a long time dead,
I'm going down that road, don't know where it goes, but the future is ahead,
I'll stop and smell a rose, I'll dance like twinkletoes, I'm gonna represent.

"You keep telling me I'm dying, but have you met me yet?"
"I will keep on fighting, and have a dance in every step,"
"You see, I'm always trying, to deny the Demon that is death,"
"You might be diagnosing, but have you met me yet?"

"You keep trying to slow me down, don't you know that I know by now?"
"You've got a pill for this and another for that, don't you know I've worked it out?"
"I'm not a fool, I'm not a sheep, I know my choices and my consequences meet,"
"You must have mistaken me for someone else... I am not one of the meek."

Now we are fast forwarding, to the year of twenty twenty five,
Yeah, I'm crystal ballin', but it's the year that I'm going to thrive,
I'm going to keep my feet on the ground, but you'll still see me fly,
Yeah, I'm crystal ballin', but it's time to celebrate this life,
I've been on my knees before, but I always knew I would rise once more,
Yeah, I'm crystal ballin', but I know I'm stronger than before,
It's time for something more, something to strive towards,
Yeah, I'm crystal ballin', you just wait and you'll see me soar.

Yeah, I'm crystal ballin', but fuck... It's a great day to be alive!

8 October, 2024

Not My Time

"Hey, Troy. Do you remember me? I am the ghost of what used to be your knees,"
"Hey, Troy. Don't forget about me! I once was your spine that didn't break or bleed,"
"Hey, Troy. Remember to breathe. I am the last part of you that is healthy,"
"Hey, Troy. Wouldn't it be easy. Just to give in, just quit and not be."

"Well, I'll tell you something, this broken body of mine,"
"You won't see me quit, while I am still alive,"
"I have much more strength, that comes from the inside,"
"So, fuck this shit, this isn't it; it's not my time to die."

People look at me and think they know, but no one knows how far I'll go,
I'll burst through the flames, bathe in the throes, I am the Hero in this show.

Pain is my companion, it lives within, so I just embrace it, with a smile and a kiss,
Turn up all the notches, watch it seep right in, it's like naughts and crosses, no one ever wins,
It can be nauseous, living in this skin, sometimes I'm over cautious, and I'm getting thin,
I know it's not your problem, nothing ever is, so don't go buy a coffin, I'm not going in.

"Hey, Troy. Do you remember me? I am the ghost of what used to be your knees,"
"Hey, Troy. Don't forget about me! I once was your spine that didn't break or bleed,"
"Hey, Troy. Remember to breathe. I am the last part of you that is healthy,"
"Hey, Troy. Wouldn't it be easy. Just to give in, just quit and not be."

"C'mon, Troy. You're better than this, you have the power to decide how you live,"
"It's all in your hands, you have got this, just raise your voice and shake your fist!'

"Well, I'll tell you something, this broken body of mine,"
"You won't see me quit, while I am still alive."
"I have much more strength, that comes from the inside,"
"So, fuck this shit, this isn't it; it's not my time to die."

The curtains won't close, the stage lights are still on,
Punches I'll throw, until all the Demons are gone,
I can do this, I know how to be strong,
These aren't the last words, you'll hear in my song.

"Hey, Troy. Do you remember me? I am the ghost of what used to be your knees,"
"Hey, Troy. Don't forget about me! I once was your spine that didn't break or bleed,"
"Hey, Troy. Remember to breathe. I am the last part of you that is healthy,"
"Hey, Troy. Wouldn't it be easy. Just to give in, just quit and not be."

"Well, I'll tell you something, this broken body of mine,"
"You won't see me quit, while I am still alive,"
"I have much more strength, that comes from the inside,"
"So, fuck this shit, this isn't it; it's not my time to die."

"Hey, Troy. Are you okay? Are you finding it hard to breathe?"
"Nah, Mate. I'm alright, I've got lots of fight left in me,"
"I'm okay, I'm just fine, I won't give up until my last breath,"
"This body of mine may be breaking, but have you met me yet?"

It's like a dance between two strangers, in such a primal way,
I was confronted with the danger, but I never was afraid,
You see, I am a fighter, and I know how to play this game,
It's like a dance between two strangers, but I will lead the way.

"Hey, Troy. Do you remember me? I am the ghost of what used to be your knees,"
"Hey, Troy. Don't forget about me! I once was your spine that didn't break or bleed,"
"Hey, Troy. Remember to breathe. I am the last part of you that is healthy,"
"Hey, Troy. Wouldn't it be easy. Just to give in, just quit and not be."

"Well, I'll tell you something, this broken body of mine,"
"You won't see me quit, while I am still alive,"
"I have much more strength, that comes from the inside,"
"So, fuck this shit, this isn't it; it's not my time to die."

21 November, 2024

Mary

Way back when this all began, I heard a doctor say,
To the lady that was in the next room, "Mary, you need to wake,"
We both had the same procedure, on the same very day,
But while I was all good, Mary was not the same.

"Mary? Mary? Wake up, Mary, it's time for you to wake,"
But Mary isn't responsive, she just won't wake.
"C'mon, Mary. Can't you hear me?" as he gives her a shake,
Mary was unlucky today, her kidney didn't take.

So now I carry Mary with me, in every step I take,
I have to earn this borrowed time, I have to stay awake.
For all the ones who didn't make it past the theatre door,
I'll fill this life so full of living there won't be room for more.

"Mary didn't make it, so, now I have to live the best,"
"Mary might have died here, but have you met me yet?"

Way back when this all began, I heard a doctor say,
To the lady that was in the next room, "Mary, you need to wake,"
We both had the same procedure, on the same very day,
But while I was all good, Mary was not the same.

"Mary? Mary? Wake up, Mary, it's time for you to wake,"
But Mary isn't responsive, she just won't wake.
"C'mon, Mary. Can't you hear me?" as he gives her a shake,
Mary was unlucky today, her kidney didn't take.

Now here I am fighting the good fight, I'm doing everything I can,
In fact it's the biggest fight of my life, but I'm no normal man.
For Mary and others like her, I'll give everything I've got left,
"Mary might have died here, but have you met me yet?"

"Hey, Troy. Are you okay? Are you finding it hard to breathe?"
"Nah, Mate. I've got this, you don't know about my inner Beast."
"You see, there's something about me, that you do not know,"
   "I've been a fighter from birth, and I can take the blows."

"Mary? Mary? Wake up, Mary, it's time for you to wake,"
   But Mary isn't responsive, she just won't wake.
"C'mon, Mary. Can't you hear me?" as he gives her a shake,
   Mary was unlucky today, her kidney didn't take.

"Mary might have died here, but I hope she's in a better place,"
"So, I remember her in my writing, and celebrate her name."

Way back when this all began, I heard a doctor say,
To the lady that was in the next room, "Mary, you need to wake,"
   We both had the same procedure, on the same very day,
   But while I was all good, Mary was not the same.

"Mary? Mary? Wake up, Mary, it's time for you to wake,"
   But Mary isn't responsive, she just won't wake.
"C'mon, Mary. Can't you hear me?" as he gives her a shake,
   Mary was unlucky today, her kidney didn't take.

"Mary might have died here, so, I will have to live my best,"
"You told me that I was dying, but have you met me yet?"

6 December, 2024

I Just Wish I Had The Words

I just wish I had the words,
To say the things I need to say,
I can only hope that you've heard,
In a kind of telepathic way.

I hope that you can feel,
That I've thought of you every day,
And I am just so grateful,
For the sacrifice that was made.

I pour the work in like a prayer,
Each day a quiet vow renewed,
A form of love I have no other way to prove,
And the family grief-drenched family who agreed.

Now I am a new man, yes,
But new the way a scar is new,
Shaped by the wound that made it,
Carved from what another man came through,
Yesterday's last breath poured into today's,
One carved out of yesterday.

All because of your sacrifice,
My life was saved,
I thank you in my heart,
Each and every day.

I just wish I had the words,
And I can only hope,
That you've heard,
In a kind of telepathic way.

I just wish I had the words,
But I hope that you've heard anyway.

21 January, 2026

This Man's Life

This man's life, it may not mean that much to others,
But I've balanced on a knife, while everyone else ran for cover,
I've always had to fight, I've had to be tougher than the others,
But that's okay, it's alright, I'm a tough mother fucker.

"Hey, Troy. Are you okay? Are you finding it hard to breathe?"
"Nah, Mate. I'm good as gold. Just take a look at me,"
"Well, we've got your latest results, and I have to say that I am impressed!"
"It was only nine months ago, when it looked like you had lost the bet,"
"No, I have just worked my arse off, to pull myself back out of the fire,"
"I reversed all of my numbers again, this disease of mine is a liar,"
"So, for all of those that doubted me, when I wasn't at my best,"
"I have got just five words for you, have you met me yet?"

I blew out all the candles on a wish I couldn't name,
Not for more time, not for less pain, just to feel some kind of flame.
That wasn't from the treatment or the fear inside my chest,
Just one more year of being more than what the doctors said was left.

"Hey, Troy. Are you okay? Are you finding it hard to breathe?"
"Nah, Mate. I'm good as gold. Just take a look at me,"
"Well, we've got your latest results, and I have to say that I am impressed!"
"It was only nine months ago, when it looked like you had lost the bet,"
"No, I have just worked my arse off, to pull myself back out of the fire,"
"I reversed all of my numbers again, this disease of mine is a liar,"
"So, for all of those that doubted me, when I wasn't at my best,"
"I have got just five words for you, have you met me yet?"

This man's life, it was never meant to be full of bliss,
But I've faced my battles, and all my Demons within,
If you think that I would stall, you have to think again,
You may think my Beast is weakness, but it is my strength.

"Sometimes, it's like a Mother that wants to smother with a pillow,"
"Sometimes, it's like the Father, that I look at in the mirror,"
"Sometimes, I wonder, well…sometimes I just wonder,"
"Sometimes, I wonder why do I have to be this man in the mirror."

This man's life, it may not mean that much to others,
But I've balanced on a knife, while everyone else ran for cover,
I've always had to fight, I've had to be tougher than the others,
But that's okay, it's alright, I'm a tough mother fucker.

"Hey, Troy. Are you okay? Are you finding it hard to breathe?"
"Nah, Mate. I'm good as gold. Just take a look at me,"
"Well, we've got your latest results, and I have to say that I am impressed!"
"It was only nine months ago, when it looked like you had lost the bet,"
"No, I have just worked my arse off, to pull myself back out of the fire,"
"I reversed all of my numbers again, this disease of mine is a liar,"
"So, for all of those that doubted me, when I wasn't at my best."
"I have got just five words for you, have you met me yet?"

This man's life….

Is to be continued….

15 December, 2024

Sing Your Own Damn Song!

There is someone very special to me that I need to mention here,
She's been through all this with me, still so young in years,
She handled all my crisis calls before she turned thirteen,
She is the light that lives in me, she is the sole reason that I breathe,
For she is my darling Daughter, she is my beautiful Kyra-Lee

"Hey, Dad. Are you okay? You know you can always rely on me,"
"You taught me how to check your work, I'm here whenever you need,"
"I know that this has been hard on you, and you're only trying to protect me,"
"When this first happened, I was only 12, but now I'm an adult, and I'm 20."

"It doesn't matter what age you are, you will always be this Dad's little girl,"
"And for as long as I live, I will try to protect you from the horrors of this world,"
"You know me, you know I'm strong. I hope my example helps you along,"
"'Cause this life can be tough, can fuck you up, but you can sing your own damn song!"

"I hope I can leave an example of someone who knew how to defy the odds,"
"I hope I can leave an example, who knew how to shake his fist against the Gods!"
"I hope I can leave an example.......of someone that you're proud of,"
"I can only hope that you remember me...................when I'm gone,"
"And I hope that you'll always remember that you can sing your own damn song!"

"Hey, Dad. Are you okay? You know you can always rely on me,"
"You taught me how to check your work, I'm here whenever you need,"
"I know that this has been hard on you, and you're only trying to protect me,"
"When this first happened I was only 12, but now I'm an adult, and I'm 20."

"It doesn't matter what age you are, you will always be this Dad's little girl,"
"And for as long as I live, I will try to protect you from the horrors of this world,"
"You know me, you know I'm strong. I hope my example helps you along,"
"'Cause this life can be tough, can fuck you up, but you can sing your own damn song!"

"Yes, this disease has challenged me, but I'll fight until my very last breath,"
"Yeah, they told me that I'm dying, but have you met me yet?"

Well, this little girl of mine, she is all grown up now,
And I am still alive today, because I had her help,
I had her checking dates and making sure I was hooked up right,
Even though I was terminal, I told her I was just fine,
There was no need to concern her, this was just my new normal,

After all, in her young eyes, her Daddy was immortal.

"Hey, Dad. Are you okay? You know you can always rely on me,"
"You taught me how to check your work, I'm here whenever you need,"
"I know that this has been hard on you, and you're only trying to protect me,"
"When this first happened, I was only 12, but now I'm an adult, and I'm 20."

"It doesn't matter what age you are, you will always be this Dad's little girl,"
"And for as long as I live, I will try to protect you from the horrors of this world,"
"You know me, you know I'm strong. I hope my example helps you along,"
"'Cause this life can be tough, can fuck you up, but you can sing your own damn song!"

"Hey, Troy. Are you okay? Are you finding it hard to breathe?"
"Nah, Mate. I'm alright. I've got my daughter who helps me,"
"She's seen it all, the scars, the tubes and all the holes in me,"
"She's seen me fall, all fucked up, and still she believes in me."

She's seen me at my weakest, then seen me defy the Gods,
When everything is bleakest, you can still sing your own damn song!

There is someone very special to me that I need to mention here,
She's been through all this with me, even though she was so young in years,
She is the light that lives in me, she is the sole reason that I breathe,
For she is my darling Daughter, she is my beautiful Kyra-Lee.

"Hey, Dad. Are you okay? You know you can always rely on me,"
"You taught me how to check your work, I'm here whenever you need,"
"I know that this has been hard on you, and you're only trying to protect me,"
"When this first happened, I was only 12, but now I'm an adult, and I'm 20."

"It doesn't matter what age you are, you will always be this Dad's little girl,"
"And for as long as I live, I will try to protect you from the horrors of this world,"
"You know me, you know I'm strong. I hope my example helps you along,"
"'Cause this life can be tough, can fuck you up, but you can sing your own damn song!"

"I hope I can leave an example.......of someone that you're proud of,"
"But most of all, I hope you remember, you can sing your own damn song!'

26 December, 2024

The Outlook

Yeah, I've been to the brink, and I've looked over the edge,
I prefer to call it the outlook, to what may lay ahead,
My future is in my hands, I know what I have to do,
I have to be the Hero in my story, only I can push on through.

It's all about perspective and how I choose to think,
Because what I prefer to call the outlook, others think of as the brink,
It's all about perspective, and knowing the skin you live in,
Yeah, what I prefer to call the outlook, others think of as the brink.

"Hey, Troy. Are you okay? Are you finding it hard to breathe,"
"To tell you the truth. There are days where I feel my fragility,"
"But I always pull through, like I do, I will always kill my weak,"
"I be, who I need to be, I pull my strength from the Beast that is me."

It's all about perspective and how I choose to think,
Because what I prefer to call the outlook, others think of as the brink,
It's all about perspective, and knowing the skin you live in,
Yeah, what I prefer to call the outlook, others think of as the brink.

Others may think about all the negatives, instead of just breathing in,
You've got to resist your hesitance, you just never can give in,
'Cause there's a whole world out there, not just what's under your skin,
Yeah, what I prefer to call the outlook, others think of as the brink.

Breathe in....breathe out....that's all you gotta do,
Breathe in....breathe out....find the truth in you,
Breathe in....breathe out....you've got nothing to prove,
Breathe in....breathe out....that's all you gotta do.

Yeah, I've been to the brink, and I've looked over the edge,
I prefer to call it the outlook, to what may lay ahead,
My future is in my hands. I know what I have to do,
I have to be the Hero in my story, only I can push on through.

It's all about perspective and how I choose to think,
Because what I prefer to call the outlook, others think of as the brink,
It's all about perspective, and knowing the skin you live in,
Yeah, what I prefer to call the outlook, others think of as the brink.

The Doctors tried to tell me I was a lost cause and I should relent,
"They might be diagnosing, but have you met me yet?"

It's all about perspective and how I choose to think,
Because what I prefer to call the outlook, others think of as the brink,
It's all about perspective, and knowing the skin you live in,
Yeah, what I prefer to call the outlook, others think of as the brink.

Yeah, what I think of as the outlook, others think of as the brink.

30 January, 2025

My Pain

"You wanna come at me, Man? Then go and shoot your shot,"
"You don't understand, Man. I'll fight with all I've got,"
"You can try and hurt me, but you'll never bring me down,"
"If you come at me, Man. You'll be the one lying on the ground."

Now I'm not talking to anyone else, I'm just talking to my pain,
It's always trying to bring me down, but I always rise again,
I am so much stronger now, I've risen from the flames,
I've risen from the concrete where the doctors left me,
I'm the weed that split the footpath, I am stronger than my pain .

"My pain tries to bring me down, but I've got lots of fight left,"
"This body of mine might be breaking down, but have you met me yet?"

My knees feel like they want to explode, right inside my legs,
They seem to be in a race of their own, the right against the left,
I can't even choose a favourite, they're both out for my death,
They've forgotten whose side they're on, so I'll just set the pace,
Finish line is getting up. The rest can keep their race."

"Hey, Troy. Are you okay? Are you finding it hard to breathe?"
"Nah, Mate. I'm alright. I won't let my pain defeat me,"
"You see, I'm much stronger than this broken body of mine,"
"My pain tries to keep me down, but I will always rise."

My knees feel like they want to explode, right inside my legs,
They seem to be in a race of their own, will the winner be the right or the left?
My back, the steel that was in my spine, is crumbling with every step,
"My pain is trying to bring me down, but have you met me yet?"

To some, it might be entertainment to see a strong man break,
But I am here to tell you that I am stronger than my pain,
I have the will, I know the fight, and I prove it every day,
Step in my shoes, try to live my life, it would probably drive you insane.

"You wanna come at me, Man? Then go and shoot your shot,"
"You don't understand, Man. I'll fight with all I've got,"
"You can try and hurt me, but you'll never bring me down,"
"If you come at me, Man. You'll be the one lying on the ground."

My knees feel like they want to explode, right inside my legs,
They seem to be in a race of their own, will the winner be the right or the left?
My back, the steel that was in my spine, is crumbling with every step,
"My pain is trying to bring me down, but have you met me yet?"

My pain is my companion now, we're intimate just like lovers,
But I will always double down, 'cause I'm one tough fucker...

2 January, 2025

Ownership

I'm all about accountability, your actions need to match your words,
That's the only judgment you'll get from me, it's simple, and it works,
I have my own personal responsibility, and I hope that you have yours,
It's all about ownership, and I own my scars, broken hearts, and hurts.

When I am down on my knees, I refuse to forgive myself for my sins,
Forgiveness for me doesn't come easy, I just own all of my shit,
It's very easy to believe that I'm only skin deep, but inside I'm broken to bits,
So, when I fuck up, I just own up. Do I really need to teach you about ownership?

All the beers I drank and all the bongs I smoked, that was always my choice,
But that was when I was young and innocent, or so everybody thought,
I own my shit, my choices were hit or miss, but when you're young, you feel immortal,
But as I age like this, I must admit, I don't get to be judgmental.

45

I've played my games, when I was living in a younger skin,
But as I've aged, I've changed, and hopefully some wisdom sunk in,
I've learned about how your life can change, in a very significant way,
But if I have failed in this life, I have only myself to blame.

I'm all about accountability, your actions need to match your words,
I wonder if there is a punishment if you don't have ownership of yourself,
I have personal responsibility, and I really hope that you have yours,
If you don't know about ownership.......what the fuck are we doing this for.

5 April, 2026

Chapter 3:
Strength

"Hey, God"

"Hey, God. I hope you're not busy, I was just wondering if you even see me,"
"I don't want to take too much of your time, prayers go unanswered, even mine,"
"I just wanted to know if you even give a fuck, or are we all just entertainment enough?"
"I want to know what channel you watch, because from here you look like a God,"
Who was invented by the loneliest people, afraid of the dark.

I know this will upset some people, but I will always stand with my principles,
The beauty of this world is oh, so simple, God is a fiction, and so is the Devil.

...God is a fiction....and so is the Devil.

This world we live in is full of sheep, the TV telecasters tell you what to think,
The government loves to sell you lies, and it's all because of political pride,
It's not about what's best for our nation, it's all about winning elections,
Now, I don't know what you think, but we are breeding a world full of sheep.

"Hey, God. I hope you're not busy, I was just wondering if you even see me,"
"I don't want to take too much of your time, prayers go unanswered, even mine,"
"I just wanted to know if you even give a fuck, or are we all just entertainment enough?"
"I want to know what channel you watch, you're just an internet hacker that we call God."

The churches, the preachers, the ones that carry your name,
They are just predators, no faith, and no shame,
"Hey, God. Why do you close your eyes?"
"Maybe, because…. you're a man-made lie…."

I've never been one who had faith, I was accountable for my own mistakes,
I've never needed an invisible crutch, I had to prove to myself that I was enough.

"Hey, God. My internet is shitty. I guess that's why, you couldn't hear me,"
"But it's all okay, I'm sitting pretty. And I've never needed someone else to heal me,"
"Now, I really don't want to be insistent, but I do have a couple of questions,"
"Like, why is there a war between different religions? Are you the real one? Is it all fiction?"
"Is Buddha a God? Is Thor even real, because if you want me to believe in you…."

I know this will upset some people, but I will always stand with my principles,
The beauty of this world is oh, so simple, God is a fiction, and so is the Devil.

…God is a fiction….and so is the Devil

"Nah, Fuck that shit. I ain't no sheep. I ain't a driver that falls asleep,"
"I've been through Hell, and I've made my way back….
And there was no God that had a thing to do with that…"

"Hey, God. I hope you're not busy, I was just wondering if you even see me,"
"I don't want to take too much of your time, prayers go unanswered, even mine,"
"I just wanted to know if you even give a fuck, or are we all just entertainment enough?"
"I want to know what channel you watch, you're just an internet hacker that we call God."

I guess there's only one thing to understand.
If there were a God, he'd lend a helping hand,
Instead, it's destruction, behind a closed eye,
"No fucking God saved me... I'm the reason I'm alive."

8 January, 2025

No Days Off

There are no days off when you're fighting for your life,
There can't be a minute wasted, it has to be done right,
You have to believe in yourself, you have to have the might,
'Cause there are no days off when you're fighting for your life.

You've gotta find your balance (I still haven't found mine),
You've gotta find your balance (But I will always try),
You've gotta find your balance (For a harmonious life),
You've gotta find your balance (I'm still searching for mine).

"Hey, Troy. Are you okay? Are you finding it hard to breathe?"
"Sure, there are times that I'm breathless, but I'm building a better me,"
"What exactly do you mean by that? What is it that you're doing?"
"I'm working my fucking arse off, there are no days off in this body that I'm building!"

Sometimes I'm the hero, and sometimes I'm the villain,
But I don't give a fuck about that, 'cause I am still livin',
I do what I have to do, I don't care about the rules I'm breakin',
To tell you the truth, some of you should take this as inspiration.

You've gotta find your balance (I still haven't found mine),
You've gotta find your balance (But I will always try),
You've gotta find your balance (For a harmonious life),
You've gotta find your balance (I'm still searching for mine).

I do have a plan for this year of twenty twenty five,
I'm going to schedule my appointments, put all my doctors in a line,
They have to learn Troy's way, I'm training them all the time,
My pain is mistreating me, but I'm the one who decides.

There are no days off when you're fighting for your life,
There can't be a minute wasted, it has to be done right,
You have to believe in yourself, you have to have the might,
'Cause there are no days off when you're fighting for your life.

My girl, my darling daughter. Has been with me all the way,
She was only twelve years old when I might have gone away,
I just put on my brave face and told her that I would be okay,
I hope I've been an example to her, to show her how to be brave,
'Cause sometimes you can be terminal, but still defy the grave...
You've just got to believe in yourself, each and every day.

I am still crystal ballin', about this future of mine,
While others might be fallin', I will only climb,
"Hang on a sec, God is callin'. He says he doesn't have the time,"
"But I am good. I'm golden. I don't need a God to keep me alive."

There are no days off, even when I feel my weakness,
Because I will never be someone who was called a victim,
I've never needed outside support, my strength comes from within me,
Because there's no one else who could handle this skin I live in.

There are no days off when you're fighting for your life,
There can't be a minute wasted, it has to be done right,
You have to believe in yourself, you have to have the might,
'Cause there are no days off when you're fighting for your life.

My burdens are my own, they don't belong to anyone else,
I've always been resistant to someone else's help,
I don't want to be seen as a victim, I need to be a champion for myself,
And I've had no days off, and that is why I am still alive now.

I don't know if this helps anyone, I'm just writing for myself,
We all have personal pains, we've all been through personal Hells,
But I know for me, it's a release that I can let out,
And I know for the rest of my life...there are no days off.

"But I am still kickin', I've got lots of life left,"
"If you ever doubted me, have you met me yet?"

You've gotta find your balance (I still haven't found mine),
You've gotta find your balance (But I will always try),
You've gotta find your balance (For a harmonious life),
You've gotta find your balance (I'm still searching for mine).

The thing about balance, it's so hard to find,
But I'll take the challenge, because I'm still alive....

When you're terminal, you're fighting for your life.
"Have you met me yet? Because I know the fight."

10 January, 2025

Mr Reaper

"Hey there, Mr Reaper. How are you today?"
"I see you've got a list there, and you're looking at my name,"
"Someone should have told you that your list is out of date,"
"'Cause I'm not going anywhere with you, no, no, not today."

I was told that I was terminal and that I couldn't be saved,
"You'll be well remembered at your memorial, it will be a lovely day,"
But I guess that they didn't know that I'm eternal, I'll defy the grave,
Because I am a born fighter, I'll always live to see another day.

I could be a rhinestone cowboy and have muscles just for show,
I can put my cowboy boots on and tip my hat so low,
I can pretend to be anyone I want, but that's just not what I do,
I am forced to live in the real world, but what about you?

"Hey there, Mr Reaper. How are you today?"
"I see you've got a list there, and you're looking at my name,"
"Someone should have told you that your list is out of date,"
"'Cause I'm not going anywhere with you, no, no, not today."

"I guess I just surpassed you, I was faster than your chase,"
"Hey there, Mr Reaper. I know how to play your game,"
"You can try and best me, but I'll smile at you with jest,"
"'Cause you are so funny to me, like, have you met me yet?"

I was told that I was terminal and that I couldn't be saved,
"You'll be well remembered at your memorial, it will be a lovely day,"
But I guess that they didn't know that I'm eternal, I'll defy the grave,
Because I am a born fighter, I'll always live to see another day.

"Hey there, Mr Reaper. I just checked your credentials,"
"It looks like you might have lapsed on the repayments for your rental,"
"Maybe you should just forget about me and focus on your life,"
"'Cause I gotta tell ya, Man, to take me down, you'll need more than a scythe."

The Devil whispers in my ear, trying to convince me that he is real,
And he sent a representative to try to seal the deal.

"Hang on a sec, what do you mean by that? Are there voices in your ear?"
"Nah, no, not at all. I'm the driver.... and he sits in the rear,"
"God is in the passenger seat, he's trying to convince me he's the real deal,"
"Yeah, I'm just a delusional guy, but guess what....I'm still here!"

I hope Mr Reaper likes to dance, 'cause I really like his flow,
But I can be the Devil in disguise, and steal his black robes,
If he wants to dance with me, he'll do it with no clothes,
Because I've been naked and abused, I know more than he knows.

"Hey there, Mr Reaper. How are you today?"
"I see you've got a list there, and you're looking at my name,"
"Someone should have told you that your list is out of date,"
"'Cause I'm not going anywhere with you, no, no, not today."

So, I am still crystal ballin', and Mr Reaper wasn't in my list,
I guess he'll have to find someone else to send to Hell instead,
I guess he doesn't know that I always fight back,
If he goes at me, I'll kill him like a heart attack.

But back to more pleasant measures, I still have fight in me,
My pain is just a tether that reminds me how to breathe.

"Hey, Troy. Are you okay? Are you finding it hard to breathe?"
"What the fuck are you talking about? Can't you see, Mr Reaper, chasing me?"
"But, I'm all good, I'm just fine. There's no Devil that can represent,"
"Mr Reaper may be chasing me, but has he met me yet?"

I've got a life to live, even though it is very limited,
I have to make smart choices, and I have to look ahead,
I have to think about the things that no one wants to think about,
"I have been to the brink...but I prefer to call it a lookout."

57

"Hey, Mr Reaper. Do you want to dance with me?"
"'Cause I can read your future, and it doesn't include me,"
"You know what they say about dancing on a grave,"
"And I'll be dancing on yours.....and there will be no name."

I was told that I was terminal and that I couldn't be saved,
"You'll be well remembered at your memorial, it will be a lovely day,"
But I guess that they didn't know that I'm eternal, I'll defy the grave,
Because I am a born fighter, I'll always live to see another day.

And if Mr Reaper wants to take me, let him join the queue,
He can wait outside the building, like the others always do.

11 January, 2025

No More Lasts

I'm all about the firsts now, there's no more lasts for me,
You can cancel the hearse now, there's still so much to see,
You can fill that hole in the dirt now, I am just gonna be me,
I've given away all my hurts now, and now I am finally free.

"Hey, Troy. Are you okay? Are you finding it hard to breathe?"
"Well, I've gotta say to you, Mate. You're kinda bugging me,"
"You see, I'm not about my last breath, I'm about the one that comes next,"
"I am not looking to the past, like, have you met me yet,"
"There's no more lasts for me, I'm all about the firsts instead,"
"Do I even have to say it again? Have you met me yet?"

I'm going to focus on my future now, maybe even chase my dreams,
I'm going to put the past behind me somehow, believe in all I can be,
The strength that I can't find within, I'll find with Nature's help,
I will just take a breath, take a moment, to just....breathe in....and breathe out.

I want to rediscover myself and commune with my younger self,
I want to let the younger me know that it is okay to ask for help.

I'm all about the firsts now, there's no more lasts for me,
You can cancel the hearse now, there's still so much to see,
You can fill that hole in the dirt now, I am just gonna be me,
I've given away all my hurts now, and now I am finally free.

We were poor when I was just a kid, and we lived in Housing Commission,
We moved a lot, from place to place, and it always felt like I didn't fit in,
Now I'm not crying about my past, I refuse, absolutely, to be called a victim,
We lived in rough areas, where it was tough, but it made me thick-skinned.

And now I have a kid of my own, well, this year she'll be twenty-one,
And I hope I have shown her that the fight's not over until you've won,
You can always have hope in your heart, but resilience comes from within,
I hope that I have been example enough to show her that she can win.

I'm all about the firsts now, there's no more lasts for me,
You can cancel the hearse now, there's still so much to see,
You can fill that hole in the dirt now, I am just gonna be me,
I've given away all my hurts now, and now I am finally free.

I'm going to put a pin in the past, and just let that old ghost ship row on by,
I'm going to live like it's my last laugh......and just go ahead and live my fucking life,
If I want to listen to Whitesnake, David Coverdale in the Still Of The Night,
I will listen as loud as I like..... because I have earned the fucking right.

"Hey, Troy. Are you okay? Are you finding it hard to breathe?"
"Well, I've gotta say to you, Mate. You're kinda bugging me,"
"You see, I'm not about my last breath, I'm about the one that comes next,"
"I am not looking to the past, like, have you met me yet?"
"There's no more lasts for me, I'm all about the firsts instead,"
"Do I even have to say it again? Have you met me yet?"

I'm all about the firsts now, there's no more lasts for me,
You can cancel the hearse now, there's still so much to see,
You can fill that hole in the dirt now, I am just gonna be me,
I've given away all my hurts now, and now I am finally free.

I'm going to leave the past behind and move on to something new,
I'm going to decide where my future lies, it's up to me to choose,
Twenty-twenty-five will be mine, because I have nothing to lose,
I'll roll the dice, do it twice, and I'll throw my hat into the ring, too.

61

It's all or nothing, or nothing at all, but this will be the first last for me,
Because I'm ignoring the craving of falling, and I am choosing me.

There's no more lasts, there's only firsts...
...because I am choosing me.

15 January, 2025

Die

And now we go back, all the way to the beginning,
When I was bombarded with info, and my head was spinning.

"Hey, Troy. How are you today? It's time that we have a chat,"
"We've been looking at your options, and we've reviewed all your labs,"
"You see, we've found some problems, and it's looking pretty bad,"
"You've only got 1% functionality, and we don't know how long you'll last,"
"We've got lots of medications, but none that will bring your kidneys back,"
"It's time for an operation, you need a Tenckhoff inserted into your abs,"
"You'll be on dialysis in the near future, while we wait for your transplant,"
"Providing you can prove that you're worth it, to take the chance."

"And now I've gotta die, die, die, die, dialyse,"
"I've gotta die, I've gotta die, I've gotta dialyse,"
"And now I've gotta die, die, die, die, dialyse,"
"I've gotta dialyse, if I want to stay alive, I've gotta dialyse,"
"I've gotta die, die, die, die, dialyse."

Draining and replacing fluids, in and out of my body, four times a day,
Doing all of my observations, recording every number on the page,
Yeah, I take this serious, there's no room for even one mistake,
And I will get myself through this, I will rise above the flames.

"And now I've gotta die, die, die, die, dialyse,"
"I've gotta die, I've gotta die, I've gotta dialyse,"
"And now I've gotta die, die, die, die, dialyse,"
"I've gotta dialyse, if I want to stay alive, I've gotta dialyse,"
"I've gotta die, die, die, die, dialyse."

Oh, great! Now I've got an infection, it's an unpleasant thing called peritonitis,
I'll tell you what, I wouldn't recommend it, it's Hell to even try to fight it,
Now there's more doses, more medications, just trying to beat this infection,
It knocked me down, so unexpected, I would beat it, and it would return with intention.

"We're very sorry to say, Troy. That your tenckhoff is blocked,"
"We'll have to remove it, we have to put you under the knife,"
"We'll wait a week or two, then we will try it again,"
"We'll put a new one in, then we'll resume with the program,"
"We've got plenty of meds to cover you until then,"
"So, there's no need for worry, you'll be right as rain."

"And now I've gotta die, die, die, die, dialyse,"
"I've gotta die, I've gotta die, I've gotta dialyse,"
"And now I've gotta die, die, die, die, dialyse,"
"I've gotta dialyse, if I want to stay alive, I've gotta dialyse,"
"I've gotta die, die, die, die, dialyse."

Now I'm on my third Tenckhoff, and guess what, it failed once again,
I'm going to need a fistula, another procedure, with my surgeon friends,
It's almost like I live here, I know all the doctors and nurses by first name,
Hey, what's another operation? We're all here, amongst friends.

For over three months, I was completely off dialysis,
I just had to wait until I had a functioning fistula,
I kept all my numbers stable, between P.D. and Haemo,
I surprised them again, no one had done this before, zero,
I am just a normal man, I'm no superhero,
But I'll never give up, because that would just be criminal.

It's been three and a half months, and now my fistula is ready for haemo,
There's no more bags for me, but they've given me a machine, though,
I plug in at night, turn out the light, hope the machine won't keep me awake,
If I do it right, I might sleep alright, as long as I don't roll the wrong way.

"And now I've gotta die, die, die, die, dialyse,"
"I've gotta die, I've gotta die, I've gotta dialyse,"
"And now I've gotta die, die, die, die, dialyse,"
"I've gotta dialyse, if I want to stay alive, I've gotta dialyse,"
"I've gotta die, die, die, die, dialyse."

This machine that I am using, it's a new one that they are trying,
They've asked me if I wanted to test it for potential problems,
Of course I was in total agreement, if there's problems I need to solve them,
If I am going to get through all this, I need to know all of the options.

"Hey, Troy. How are you today? It's time that we have a chat,"
"We've been looking at your options, and we've reviewed all your labs,"
"You see, we've found some problems, and it's looking pretty bad,"
"You've only got 1% functionality, and we don't know how long you'll last,"
"We've got lots of medications, but none that will bring your kidneys back,"
"It's time for an operation, you need a Tenckhoff inserted into your abs,"
"You'll be on dialysis in the near future, while we wait for your transplant,"
"Providing you can prove that you're worth it, to take the chance."

From diagnosis to transplant, it was two years and thirteen days,
It was a hard road that I travelled, but I've made it to today.

"For all of those doubters who thought I had nothing left,"
"I've only got five words for you, have you met me yet?"

"And now I've gotta die, die, die, die, dialyse,"
"I've gotta die, I've gotta die, I've gotta dialyse",
"And now I've gotta die, die, die, die, dialyse,"
"I've gotta dialyse, if I want to stay alive, I've gotta dialyse,"
"I've gotta die, die, die, die, dialyse."

"And now I've gotta die, die, die, die, dialyse,"
"I've gotta die, I've gotta die, I've gotta dialyse,"
"And now I've gotta die, die, die, die, dialyse,"
"I've gotta dialyse, if I want to stay alive, I've gotta dialyse,"
"I've gotta die, die, die, die, dialyse."

Now the title might be "Die", but it's all about staying alive,
Forget about sins and pride, it's about having an open mind,
I don't love the fight, but I can fight to stay alive,
They said I was gonna die, but here I am now, saying, "Hi."

"For all of those who didn't believe in me and thought I had lost the bet,"
"I still only have five words for you, have you met me yet?"

17 January, 2025

Move More

"Move more so you can move more", it's one of the things I say to myself,
Do more, so you can do more, this whole damn life of mine has been a workout,
I'll prove myself, to only myself, I don't need anyone's shadows of doubt,
If I want help, I'll help myself, these are my burdens, my own personal Hell.

I'll dance like I own the dancefloor, regardless of all my pain,
I'll dance inside the downpour, "Oh, Lord, let it rain!"

Energy doesn't disappear, it just turns into something else,
I have no idea what is next, but I'm willing to wait it out,
I can be patient if I need to, even though I need answers now,
I can be what I need to be, I'm the chameleon now.

"Hey, Troy. Are you okay? You're looking kinda tired,"
"Yeah, I guess I'm alright. But my body feels like it's on fire,"
"What's going on, Troy? Tell me what's happening to you,"
"Well, I guess my body is falling apart, but I will push on through."

"Move more so you can move more", it's one of the things I say to myself,
Do more, so you can do more, this whole damn life of mine has been a workout,
I'll prove myself, to only myself, I don't need anyone's shadows of doubt,
If I want help, I'll help myself, these are my burdens, my own personal Hell.

"Be more so you can be more", just another thing that I tell myself,
Sure, I've got a slogan of four, but these are things that chase my Demons out,
I've got all the tools, even though most of them are old and broken,
Maybe I'm just a fool, and my future is already written.

"But, while I still draw breath, I will always defy my death,"
"'Cause the Reaper may be chasing, but has he met me yet?"
"Hey, God. What are you thinking? Should I just relent?"
"Nah, I'm only kidding, after all, have you met me yet?"

My shoulder feels like it wants to fall off, so I lift a heavier weight instead,
'Cause there are absolutely no days off, and the real battle is in my head,
It is all about perspective, and the way that I choose to think,
Because what I prefer to call the outlook, others think of it as the brink.

"Move more so you can move more", it's one of the things I say to myself,
Do more, so you can do more, this whole damn life of mine has been a workout,
I'll prove myself, to only myself, I don't need anyone's shadows of doubt,
If I want help, I'll help myself, these are my burdens, my own personal Hell.

I am a champion, I am a fucking star,
Not because of talent, just because I work hard,
I do much more than those who are ten years younger,
Because I have got the drive in me, I can feel the hunger.

There are no days off when you're fighting for your life,
You have to move your body and exercise your mind,
You have to do what works for you, in a way that feels right,
But, for me, I never give up, because I know this fight.

I'll dance like I own the dancefloor, regardless of all my pain,
I'll dance inside the downpour, "Oh, Lord, let it rain!"

"Move more so you can move more", it's one of the things I say to myself,
Do more, so you can do more, this whole damn life of mine has been a workout,
I'll prove myself, to only myself, I don't need anyone's shadows of doubt,
If I want help, I'll help myself, these are my burdens, my own personal Hell.

"And this disease ain't killing me...
...'cause I'm a completely different kind of beast."

18 January, 2025

A Completely Different Kind of Beast

"You haven't met someone like me, I'm a completely different kind of beast,"
"I will fight with every part of me, I am stronger than this damn disease,"
"I refuse to live my life on my knees, yeah, I ain't here to please,"
"I am fighting with all the strength that's in me, I'm a completely different kind of beast."

Yeah, they said, "Troy, you're going to die, in fact, we're amazed that you're still alive!"
But they don't know me, they don't know that... in the garden of adversity, I always thrive!
Seed me, weed me, poison my pride, I am the unnatural growth that stays alive,
Feed me, bleed me, drain me of my life,
To end me, you'll need more than a scythe.

My previous weaknesses are a stepping stone to what comes next,
I've learned from my mistakes, and I am owning what life I have left,
From those weaknesses, I draw strength, because I am stronger than my pain,
All those experiences that I've been in, they are the creator of my beast.

"You haven't met someone like me, I'm a completely different kind of Beast,"
"I will fight with every part of me, I am stronger than this damn disease,"
"I refuse to live my life on my knees, yeah, I ain't here to please,"
"I am fighting with all the strength that's in me, I'm a completely different kind of Beast."

"Hey, Troy. Are you okay? Are you finding it hard to breathe?"
"Nah, Mate. I am golden. I've brought along my Beast,"
"You see, he is my champion, my guardian, when I am feeling weak,"
"And when I cannot do for myself, he always protects me,"
"In fact, if you really want to know, he is me... and I am my Beast,"
"Yes, you heard me right. I am him... and my Beast is me."

"You haven't met someone like me, I'm a completely different kind of Beast,"
"I will fight with every part of me, I am stronger than this damn disease,"
"I refuse to live my life on my knees, yeah, I ain't here to please,"
"I am fighting with all the strength that's in me, I'm a completely different kind of Beast."

There's no bridge that crosses time, there's no button to press rewind,
I just have to live my life......along with this Beast.....that I call mine.

I've seen Beasts before, in other men's eyes,
While they cage theirs, I will always embrace mine,
They can medicate themselves, ignore their own lies,
I prefer to release my Beast, because that is how I thrive.

There's no bridge that crosses time, there's no button to press rewind,
I just have to live my life......along with this Beast.....that I call mine.

"You haven't met someone like me, I'm a completely different kind of Beast,"
"I will fight with every part of me, I am stronger than this damn disease,"
"I refuse to live my life on my knees, yeah, I ain't here to please,"
"I am fighting with all the strength that's in me, I'm a completely different kind of Beast."

18 January, 2025

To My Very Last Breath

I will fight, I will fight, I will fight... to my very last breath,
Every day, every night, of my life... I will defy my death,
I will be what I need, I'll be the knife... that cuts through the dread,
I am here, I am upright, I have survived..."Have you met me yet?"

"Hey, Troy. Are you okay? Are you finding it hard to breathe?"
"Nah, Mate. I'm alright. There has never been a quitter in me,"
"I know this fight, and what it takes. There's no room for mistakes,"
"I'll be the light, forget about hate. 'Cause I'm the decider of my fate."

Well, guess what? I'll be wearing purple again tomorrow,
There's more bits to be cut out of me, but really, there's not much left though,
For the last two days, I've weighed the lowest of my adult life,
62.7 kilos. You can play my ribs like an accordion, and record it on an audio file.

I will fight, I will fight, I will fight... to my very last breath,
Every day, every night, of my life... I will defy my death,
I will be what I need, I'll be the knife... that cuts through the dread,
I am here, I am upright, I have survived..."Have you met me yet?"

I will make a deal with my surgeons, like I always do,
"Just don't kill me on the table, and I won't die on you,"
Sure, we'll have a laugh, it's really just something to lighten the mood,
And when I go under the knife, I insist that I'm listening to '80's tunes,
"So, don't kill me on the table, or I'll fucking haunt you,"
"Nah, I'm only kidding, it's just my funny jokes,"
"But, seriously, if you kill me.........I'd check your brakes aren't broke,"
"Nah, really, I'm only mucking about, but you'd better be a Superstar tomorrow."

It's my life that's on the line every time that I go under the knife,
If a surgeon makes a mistake, he'll still go back to his home tonight,
I might be in the morgue, as they're cooling my body like ice,
Or I might be on a respirator for the rest of my entire damn life.

I will fight, I will fight, I will fight... to my very last breath,
Every day, every night, of my life... I will defy my death,
I will be what I need, I'll be the knife... that cuts through the dread,
I am here, I am upright, I have survived..." Have you met me yet?"

"You've got a pill for this, a drug for that, and everything in between,"
"C'mon now, let's tell the truth, there's no profit in curing me."

I've got my body age down to 44 years of age, and my bodily muscle is 75.7%,
So, through all this, I've been able to lose a decade, and fucking represent,
"So, to all those doubters, those ones that thought I didn't have anything left,"
"I've still got those same five words for you, have you met me yet?"

I will fight, I will fight, I will fight... to my very last breath,
Every day, every night, of my life... I will defy my death,
I will be what I need, I'll be the knife... that cuts through the dread,
I am here, I am upright, I have survived..."Have you met me yet?"

I will fight to my last goddamn breath, because the hard way is all I know,
This life can throw its fists at me, but I've always been able to take the blows,
I've never been one to follow the trends, I do things my own way,
There's no need to be in competition with me, you couldn't compete anyway.

"So, now here I am talking to you. Because tomorrow has no promises to prove,"
"I will do everything I can do, to survive the day, just like I always do,"
"But, just in case something goes wrong tomorrow, and I meet my end,"
"I would say, don't believe that shit, like, have you met me yet?"

I will fight, I will fight, I will fight… to my very last breath,
Every day, every night, of my life… I will defy my death,
I will be what I need, I'll be the knife… that cuts through the dread,
I am here, I am upright, I have survived…"Have you met me yet?"

I will fight, I will fight, I will fight… to my very last breath,
Every day, every night, of my life… I will defy my death,
I will be what I need, I'll be the knife… that cuts through the dread,
I am here, I am upright, I have survived…"Have you met me yet?"

27 January, 2025

Chapter 4:
No Excuses

Kidneyman

Now there's something you might not know about us, transplant patients,
When we get an organ donation, sometimes we like to name them,
One lady named her kidney, 'Daisy,' while one guy went with, 'Batman,'
Me, I'm a little different to them, I named mine, 'Nichole Kidneyman!'

To win this game, you can't be the same as everyone else,
You've gotta do it your own way, be the Beast that helps himself,
Be the King or the Queen who believes in themselves,
You can do it all, or be the fall, I guess you have to decide for yourself.

"Hey, Troy. Are you okay? Are you finding it hard to breathe?"
"C'mon, Guys. You know me. I am not one who believes in defeat,"
"But, c'mon, Troy. Sometimes you have got to have your doubts,"
"Have you even met me yet?. I'm the Kidneyman, Nic always helps me out."

I am the Kidneyman, Nic is always on my side,
She is my lifeblood, and I praise her, I've survived,
She is my partner in crime, she is my steely knife,
She don't know shit about me, but I thought she wouldn't mind,
Sure, I ain't no one that she would know about....
...But because of my kidney transplant...I am still alive,
And that is why I named my kidney...
...Nichole Kidneyman... and we are side by side.

Now there's something you might not know about us transplant patients,
When we get an organ donation, sometimes we like to name them,
One lady named her kidney, 'Daisy,' while one guy went with, 'Batman,'
Me, I'm a little different to them, I named mine, 'Nichole Kidneyman!'

I guess what in the end that I am saying, you have the strength inside,
You just have to do what you have to do if you want to stay alive,
Nichole Kidman don't know shit about me, but that's alright,
It's called breathing in and breathing out, it's about staying alive.

I gave my kidney a funny name because that's how I roll,
But I take this seriously though, I'm the one in control,
But I have always appreciated the one who held my hand,
Because of my donation, I have to live my life and expand,
I don't mean to diminish the one who extended my life,
I will always appreciate her, she fucking saved my life.

Now the baton has been passed, and I know what I need to do,
I have to be the Kidneyman, I've still got lots to prove.

Now there's something you might not know about us transplant patients,
When we get an organ donation, sometimes we like to name them,
One lady named her kidney, 'Daisy,' while one guy went with, 'Batman,'
Me, I'm a little different to them, I named mine, 'Nichole Kidneyman!'

I am the Kidneyman, Nic is always on my side,
She is my lifeblood, and I praise her, I've survived,
She is my partner in crime, she is my steely knife,
She don't know shit about me, but I thought she wouldn't mind,
Sure, I ain't no one that she would know about...
...But because of my kidney transplant... I am still alive,
And that is why I named my kidney...
...Nichole Kidneyman... and we are side by side.

4 February, 2025

Fragility

It's not like me to admit my fragility, but I can't always be the man of steel,
I have a weakness that breeds in me, but I can be honest about how I feel,
Like, I've gotta say, these last couple of years, they have been a real challenge,
But, I don't get on my knees, I face my fears, I will soar like the mighty falcon.

It can be hard to be strong all day long, and then again into the night,
But I sing my own damn song, to carry me along, I am ready for this fight,
Even though my pain tries to bring me down, I just do the work,
Mr Reaper's been around, like a dark cloud, but I am stronger than my hurts.

I am stronger, I am worse, I can survive these invisible hurts,
I won't linger, for the hearse, you can fill that hole in the dirt.

It's not like me to admit my fragility, but I can't always be the man of steel,
I have a weakness that breeds in me, but I can be honest about how I feel,
Like, I've gotta say, these last couple of years, they have been a real challenge,
But I don't get on my knees, I face my fears, and I refuse to believe,
That I won't create a better me,
I will face the challenge, find the balance, embrace what I need
I will do every Goddamn thing that I need,
I face my fears, I will find a way to soar.

"Hey, Troy. Are you okay? Are you finding it hard to breathe?"
"Even though your numbers look great, I can sense some fragility,"
"Well, I gotta tell ya, I've faced my challenges like a million-dollar bet,"
"Like, you don't even know me, have you met me yet?"

Well, what can I say? I'm 54 years old, quickly closing in 55,
And some days are so much harder to sustain the fight,
My body likes to deny me, but I never give it the chance,
'Cause one day I'll be dying, so I am going to fucking dance.

It's not like me to admit my fragility, but I can't always be the man of steel,
I have a weakness that breeds in me, but I can be honest about how I feel,
Like, I've gotta say, these last couple of years, they have been a real challenge,
But, I don't get on my knees, I face my fears, I will soar like the mighty falcon.

I had another procedure last week, and I guess you could say it rocked me,
I got home and was all trembly and weak, and nothing would stay down in me,
I had chills from my head to my feet, and I was lacking in clarity,
And there was only one person who looked after me...my darling daughter, Kyra-Lee.

It is okay to admit pain, it's also fine to ask for help,
You don't have to do it alone, you can always reach out,
But that's not the way I do things, I have to do it myself,
Because when it all comes down to it. Am I a man? Or am I a mouse?

All this pain that lives in me, I use it to feed my Beast,
Even though I have fragility, you'll never see it in me.

It's not like me to admit my fragility, but I can't always be the man of steel,
I have a weakness that breeds in me, but I can be honest about how I feel,
Like, I've gotta say, these last couple of years, they have been a real challenge,
But, I don't get on my knees, I face my fears, I will soar like the mighty falcon.

All of this fragility, it is mine and for no one else,
All these burdens that I carry, I just can't put them down....

6 February, 2025

Prisoner Number

I have got these jailhouse blues, in this hospital where I live,
I'm not here 24/7, but sometimes it feels like I should move in,
This past decade has challenged me, but I will never give in,
Sure, I have a patient I.D., but my prisoner number is...
...One-three-six...two-six-six....

Yeah, I know it kinda sounds stupid, but when you've been at this for as long as I have,
I'm always working towards improvement, but sometimes it feels there's no way out,
I know I have free movement, but I am still shackled just the same,
It wasn't any of my choosing, and it is such a wicked, wicked game.

I was always better as an outpatient than as a patient within,
The hospital system gets me frustrated, it's like I've committed a cardinal sin,
It's almost like a penalisation if you fight the fight and happen to win,
They prefer my hospitalisation, but there's no cage that you can put me in.

"Hey, Troy. Are you okay? Are you finding it hard to breathe?'
"Breathing was never the problem for me. It was your lack of belief,"
"But, that's okay. It's all just fine. Every day is like winning a million-dollar bet,"
"But you wouldn't know that about me, like, have you met me yet?"

I have got these jailhouse blues, in this hospital where I live,
I'm not here 24/7, but sometimes it feels like I should move in,
This past decade has challenged me, but I will never give in,
Sure, I have a patient I.D., but my prisoner number is…
…One-three-six…two-six-six….

Now, that's not my real patient I.D. I'd be a fool to put that in script,
So, I just chose some numbers for me that have relevance instead,
The first three numbers are my diagnosis date,
The second three numbers are the day I was saved,
And if you work out the difference, it's a total of 2 years and 13 days.

Yeah, I know it kinda sounds stupid, but when you've been at this for as long as I have,
I'm always working towards improvement, but sometimes it feels there's no way out,
I know I have free movement, but I am still shackled just the same,
It wasn't any of my choosing, and it is such a wicked, wicked game.

I have got these jailhouse blues, in this hospital where I live,
I'm not here 24/7, but sometimes it feels like I should move in,
This past decade has challenged me, but I will never give in,
Sure, I have a patient I.D., but my prisoner number is...
...One-three-six...two-six-six....

Sure, I have a patient I.D., but my prisoner number is.......

9 February, 2025

Movement is My Medicine

Movement is my medicine, it's the reason that I have survived,
Everything I do is exercise, to keep this beating heart alive,
Nothing is irrelevant, I look at all of my stats in detail,
I have got a hold of this, and it's just not in my nature to fail.

"Move more so you can move more", that's something that I tell myself,
"Do more so you can do more." Do I really have to spell it out?
I'll be more, so I can be more, there's more to this world than just myself,
I'll learn more so I can know more. My first priority is my health.

It's not my place to tell you what to do, I can only tell you what I went through,
I could have succumbed, and in the end just relinquish myself,
But I was up for the fight, and I knew without a doubt…
There's only one person in this world that can save me……and that is myself.

Movement is my medicine, it's what I've got to do,
There's no point in being reticent, I just have to move,
Everything else is irrelevant, I've got just one life to lose,
So, I'm the one who will be telling it about how I pulled through.

"You've got a drug for this, a pill for that, in fact, I can see your prescription pad,"
"Your pen is out, you're ready to write down anything that will show me out,"
"It's big business that you're in. Don't you ever worry about all your sins?"
"C'mon, Troy. We're only trying to help you out. Why do you always present with doubt?"
"It's really simple, no one knows me better than myself. I will decide when I check out,"
"You've had your chances, and you've fucked up a lot. So, I am here to save myself."

Movement is my medicine, it's the reason that I have survived,
Everything I do is exercise, to keep this beating heart alive,
Nothing is irrelevant, I look at all of my stats in detail,
I have got a hold of this, and it's just not in my nature to fail.

I try so hard to be strong, and I keep a record of all my stats,
"I will sing my own damn song! And to tell you the truth. Fuck everyone else,"
"I am the one who has to be strong, have you ever had a moment of real pain?"
"Because I can guarantee you, you can diagnose, but you can't play this game."

Yeah, I've had my bitch. I think that I'm allowed to express my pain,
But, I gotta tell ya, when you've got an itch, you've got to believe in your flame,
'Cause when you're terminal, you have to find your own way,
I know for me personally, I had to chase Mr Reaper away.

"Move more so you can move more", that's something that I tell myself,
"Do more so you can do more," do I really have to spell it out?
I'll be more, so I can be more, there's more to this world than just myself,
I'll learn more so I can know more, my first priority is my health.

Movement is my medicine, it's the reason that I have survived,
Everything I do is exercise, to keep this beating heart alive,
Nothing is irrelevant, I look at all of my stats in detail,
I have got a hold of this, and it's just not in my nature to fail.

And one final thing, "Have you met me yet?"

9 February, 2025

Golden

"Hey, Troy. Are you okay? Are you finding it hard to breathe?"
"Nah, Mate. I am golden. I'm as golden as can be,"
"One thing you might not know about me, I can bend and break and bleed,"
"But here I am, look at me. I am alive, and I am still standing."

Sure, I have pain, it's a part of me, but I'm stronger than my hurts,
I refuse to live on my knees, I do believe that I still have worth,
Not only for me, but for my community, anyone who's gone through Hell,
Open your eyes, and you will see, we all have our own story to tell.

Mr Reaper, you see, he's been chasing me,
But when it comes to death, I'm Speedy Gonzalez,
He can come for me, but I'm faster than his chase,
If he wants to take the chance, it's he who will be laid to waste.

There are days that are harder because of this damn disease,
But I respond with laughter, 'cause nothing's stronger than my Beast,
He is my undercover, and it is he who grants me release,
'Cause I'm not going under, I'm stronger than this disease.

"Hey, Troy. Are you okay? Are you finding it hard to breathe?"
"Nah, Mate. I am golden. I'm as golden as can be,"
"One thing you might not know about me, I can bend and break and bleed,"
"But here I am, look at me. I am alive, and I am still standing."

I don't really need anyone else's faith, I have faith enough in myself,
I'll have wins, and I'll make mistakes, and you'll never hear me ask for help.

I am golden, I'm living hard,
I am golden, I'm dropping the past,
I am golden, so beats my heart,
I am golden, mine is the last laugh.

There's no reception area in the waiting room of the afterlife,
So, I will spend my life right here, still enduring the fight,
I am living each day like I won a million-dollar bet,
You might wonder why I say this, "but have you met me yet?"

Sure, I have pain, it's a part of me, but I'm stronger than my hurts,
I refuse to live on my knees, I do believe that I still have worth,
Not only for me, but for my community, anyone who's gone through Hell,
Open your eyes, and you will see, we all have our own story to tell.

"Hey, Troy. Are you okay? Are you finding it hard to breathe?"
"Nah, Mate. I am golden. I'm as golden as can be,"
"One thing you might not know about me, I can bend and break and bleed,"
"But here I am, look at me. I am alive, and I am still standing."

10 February, 2025

Fighting Back

Verbal instructions, being thrown like punches, this life of mine knows the pain,
Character destruction, just like cut lunches, there's a new fight every day,
When I can't function, and I'm going under, and I think that it's all in my brain,
"Excuse the interruption, your program will return soon," I better just stay in my lane.

I can't do it right now, I'm in the wrong crowd, but it's a crowd of only one,
I hear the wrong sounds, they're in my head now, maybe I'm finally done,
I need the right choice, give me the right voice, but somehow I'm always wrong,
Visiting the black void, covered in white noise, I can't find my song,
But, I will write much more, I know what I fight for, 'til my very last breath,
And I know what I'll die for, and stay alive for, "like, have you met me yet?"

All these distractions, massive overreactions, will I ever find my peace?
Breaking down into fractions, rising to the challenge, searching for some release,
Character assassination, over manipulation, judged right to the nth degree,
Lack of imagination, overstimulation, I'm so confused. Who should I be?

"Hey, Troy. Are you okay? Are you finding it hard to breathe?"
"Nah, Mate. I am golden. You'll never see me on my knees,"
"I've gotta tell ya, I know this fight, it's one I've been fighting all of my life,"
"So, if you want to ask me if I am alright, just remember, I just don't die."

I can't do it right now, I'm in the wrong crowd, but it's a crowd of only one,
I hear the wrong sounds, they're in my head now, maybe I'm finally done,
I need the right choice, give me the right voice, but somehow I'm always wrong,
Visiting the black void, covered in white noise, I can't find my song,
But, I will write much more, I know what I fight for, 'til my very last breath,
And I know what I'll die for, and stay alive for, "like, have you met me yet?"

Verbal instructions, being thrown like punches, this life of mine knows the pain,
Character destruction, just like cut lunches, there's a new fight every day,
When I can't function, and I'm going under, and I think that it's all in my brain,
"Excuse the interruption, your program will return soon," I better just stay in my lane.

All these distractions, massive overreactions, will I ever find my peace?
Breaking down into fractions, rising to the challenge, searching for some release,
Character assassination, over manipulation, judged right to the nth degree,
Lack of imagination, overstimulation, I'm so confused. Who should I be?

Searching for salvation, over this frustration, is it all a fucking game?
Sleeping at train stations, dealing with starvation, while the fat cats have their way,
I'm over this inaction, over medication, we should hang our heads in shame,
Broken communication, over legislation, here you go, sign your life away.

"Hey, Troy. How have you been? We haven't seen you for a while,"
"Well, I've been busy, really busy. I've had to double down to win this fight,"
"Oh, okay, what's been happening? I've seen your numbers, and they are great,"
"Oh, you think you had something to do with that? Well, I guess that's your mistake,"
"I put in the work, I worked real hard. Even when it felt like my body was falling apart,"
"Because I don't give in, I don't give up. I will decide when my number is up!"

Verbal instructions, being thrown like punches, this life of mine knows the pain,
Character destruction, just like cut lunches, there's a new fight every day,
When I can't function, and I'm going under, and I think that it's all in my brain,
"Excuse the interruption, your program will return soon," I better just stay in my lane.

I can't do it right now, I'm in the wrong crowd, but it's a crowd of only one,
I hear the wrong sounds, they're in my head now, maybe I'm finally done,
I need the right choice, give me the right voice, but somehow I'm always wrong,
Visiting the black void, covered in white noise, I can't find my song,
But, I will write much more, I know what I fight for, 'til my very last breath,
And I know what I'll die for, and stay alive for, "like, have you met me yet?"

It's not like me to admit my fragility, but I can't always be the man of steel,
But I know how to bleed, rise from my knees, yet be honest about how I feel,
Now I am stronger, now I am worse, but I can survive these invisible hurts,
I will not linger, just cancel the hearse. While you're at it, you can fill that hole in the dirt.

All these distractions, massive overreactions, will I ever find my peace?
Breaking down into fractions, rising to the challenge, searching for some release,
Character assassination, over manipulation, judged right to the nth degree,
Lack of imagination, overstimulation, I'm so confused. Who should I be?

I can't do it right now, I'm in the wrong crowd, but it's a crowd of only one,
I hear the wrong sounds, they're in my head now, maybe I'm finally done,
I need the right choice, give me the right voice, but somehow I'm always wrong,
Visiting the black void, covered in white noise, I can't find my song,
But, I will write much more, I know what I fight for, 'til my very last breath,
And I know what I'll die for, and stay alive for, "like, have you met me yet?"

I live my life every day and night, doing what I think is best for me,
And then something come right out of the blue, there was this epiphany,
Now I don't really love the fight, but I know it like the back of my hand,
And that I was never really fighting, I was only ever fighting back.

17 February, 2025

Million Dollar Bet

"Yeah, this life of mine has been a fight, but I ain't nowhere near dead,"
"For Mr Reaper, I'll smile tonight, 'cause he hasn't been able to catch me yet,"
"I am living every day and every night, just like I won a million dollar bet,"
"You might think you know me, but like, have you met me yet?"

I'll throw the die, I'll play this game, my hat is right in the ring,
I will survive, you'll remember my name, 'cause I just don't give in,
This roulette wheel, it spins again, all my chips are in,
I know the deal, I've played this game, and I will always win.

"Hey, Troy. Are you okay? Are you finding it hard to breathe?"
"Nah, Mate. I'm quite alright. I know there are no days off for me,"
"This casino of life, on the edge of a knife, I'll bring the House to its knees,"
"If you like, you can place a bet tonight. As long as you place all your bets on me."

"Yeah, this life of mine has been a fight, but I ain't nowhere near dead,"
"For Mr Reaper, I'll smile tonight, 'cause he hasn't been able to catch me yet,"
"I am living every day and every night, just like I won a million dollar bet,"
"You might think you know me, but like, have you met me yet?"

"Hey, God. How are you doing? You haven't had much to say,"
"Oh, yeah. I forgot you're busy, ruling some other planet in space,"
"But that's alright, I'm always improving, I don't need you to save the day,"
"So, while you're there, being busy, I'll take charge of this game."

I'll throw the die, I'll play this game, my hat is right in the ring,
I will survive, you'll remember my name, 'cause I just don't give in,
This roulette wheel, it spins again, all my chips are in,
I know the deal, I've played this game, and I will always win.

I will play you in poker, with my last single cent,
'Cause I am living, like I won a million dollar bet,
I might be hoping, but I ain't spent yet,
Every day above ground is like winning a million dollar bet.

In the end, there's no luck, it's all about the work,
If you don't give a fuck, you'll only get worse,
But I'm tough enough to crawl out of the dirt,
Yeah, I'm tough enough to survive this world.

"Yeah, this life of mine has been a fight, but I ain't nowhere near dead,"
"For, Mr Reaper, I'll smile tonight, 'cause he hasn't been able to catch me yet,"
"I am living every day and every night, just like I won a million dollar bet,"
"You might think you know me, but like, have you met me yet?"

There are no excuses, no days off, when you're fighting for your life,
Sometimes I lose it, only to regain it, because I know how to survive,
There's no promise that can't be broken, so I rely on me, myself and I,
A misdiagnosis, an unfollowed process, could be the end of my life.

I'll throw the die, I'll play this game, my hat is right in the ring,
I will survive, you'll remember my name, 'cause I just don't give in,
This roulette wheel, it spins again, all my chips are in,
I know the deal, I've played this game, and I will always win.

"Yeah, this life of mine has been a fight, but I ain't nowhere near dead,"
"For, Mr Reaper, I'll smile tonight, 'cause he hasn't been able to catch me yet,"
"I am living every day and every night, just like I won a million dollar bet,"
"You might think you know me, but like, have you met me yet?"

But I am stronger, even though I'm older, because I'll never forget,
There are people who think of it as the brink, but I prefer to call it the outlook instead,
It's okay to falter, but you can go on, just believe in your heart and your head,
Because for me, every day living is like I won a million dollar bet.

17 February, 2025

Exactly Where I'm Supposed To Be

Yeah, I know you've heard it all before, but hear me out one more time,
A man who's still standing where they said he wouldn't be,
Travelling a road that should have broken me,

And finding out it took me exactly where I'm supposed to be.

I have worked so hard, so hard that you wouldn't believe,
I have put in the work, knowing that I would succeed,
They gave me 1%, it was the death penalty for me,
But what they didn't know is that I believe in me.

This road that I have travelled has definitely not been easy,
But it took me, yeah, it took me to......exactly where I'm supposed to be,
This path that I have paved, with every setback and every scar,
It took me, yeah, it took me to...exactly where I'm supposed to be..

Now here I stand in the year 2025, it was nine years ago that they said,
"Hey, Troy. Don't you know that you're going to die?"
"In fact, we're all amazed that you are still alive,"
What they didn't know, in the garden of adversity, I will always thrive.

"Hey, Troy. Are you okay? Are you finding it hard to breathe?"
"Nah, Mate. I'm alright. I'm exactly where I'm supposed to be,"
"You guys never had faith in me, so I kept you out of my head,"
"I was always going to beat this thing, have you met me yet?"

My body feels like a skin bag that's full of broken bits,
But there are no excuses to be had, I just have to rise above it,
I'll reach right in, deep inside of me, get my strength from my Beast,
I don't give in, it's just not me, I will fight with every last part of me.

"You've got a drug for this, a drug for that, and everything in between,"
"I'll just take the minimum, thanks. My Beast is all I need."

Yeah, I know you've heard it all before, all about how Troy will soar,
I'm sure it's boring, to you and yours, but this guy has got lots to live for,
Of course you have the option, of not reading these anymore,
But I write this for me, not for you, I'm sorry if you are bored,
And it's just like I said before, this is my release, I hope you can find yours,
It's not a competition, it's just about me, there's no one else that's keeping score.

This road that I have travelled, has definitely not been easy,
But it took me, yeah, it took me to...exactly where I'm supposed to be,
This path that I have paved, with my blood, sweat and tears,
It took me, yeah, it took me to...exactly where I'm supposed to be.

In the end, here's where I stand...I'm exactly where I'm supposed to be.

23 February, 2025

Adapt or Die

There is no question, there is no wondering why,
It is quite a simple thing, it's just a case of adapt or die,
When every single day is a fight, a fight just to stay alive,
It really is a simple thing, it's just a case of adapt or die.

Break down the numbers, examine them to the nth,
"It's not looking good, Troy.", "Have you met me yet?"
Maybe I'm not a good boy, maybe I'm not the best,
Some may like to destroy, but I'm not like the rest,
I will always make the right choice, I will never relent,
I will listen to my own voice, "Have you met me yet?"

There are no excuses, in case you're wondering why,
I fight this fight with purpose, to keep myself alive,
Because I know I'm worth it, I will always fight,
Even though I am hurting, it's just a case of adapt or die.

There is no question, there is no wondering why,
It is quite a simple thing, it's just a case of adapt or die,
When every single day is a fight, a fight just to stay alive,
It really is a simple thing, it's just a case of adapt or die.

This busted and broken body of mine, it likes to betray me,
Every chance it gets, it tries, it thinks that it can blame me,
But I am the reason I'm alive, my mind is stronger than my knees,
Whilst I am still standing upright, I will always have belief.

Mr Reaper has his sights on me, but I am faster than his chase,
He is just a liability, he's a distraction that I lay to waste,
I tried to speak to God, but he was unavailable today,
Maybe the line went dead, or maybe there was nothing there to say.

"Hey, Troy. Are you okay? Are you finding it hard to breathe?
"Nah, Mate. I do what I do. To keep this living heart beating,"
"But, if you really want to offer some help, how about listening to me?"
"You're just too busy saying this and that, you're just talking at me!"

There is no question, there is no wondering why,
It is quite a simple thing, it's just a case of adapt or die,
When every single day is a fight, a fight just to stay alive,
It really is a simple thing, it's just a case of adapt or die.

There is no question, there is no wondering why,
I am the answer, I am the proof of adapt or die.

23 February, 2025

No Excuses

There are no excuses, you can never just relent,
You've got to know your purpose, you've got to live your best,
This life can be a circus, can mess you up in the head,
But I know that I'm worth it, "like, have you met me yet?"

First I stumble, then I fall, my face is on the tiled bathroom floor,
I take a second, breathe it in, I've been this low before,
The grout lines at eye level, the humming of the light,
Then I put my hands beneath me,
that is how I fight,
The stairs aren't my friends when my knees disappear,
My back wants to crumble, yeah, this shit is real,
But there are no excuses, I'll always get up again.

"Of course you don't believe me, but have you met me yet?"

Everything that has happened has led me right to here,
It wasn't something that was planned, but I face it without fear,
I don't care about the clowns that tell me I'm gonna die,
Because I am more than happy to tell them I'm still alive.

There are no excuses, you obviously haven't met me yet,
Every day above ground is like winning a million dollar bet,
But I don't like to gamble, if I did, I would put every bet on me,
I don't care about being humble, it's all about the ability to breathe.

First I stumble, then I fall, my face is on the tiled bathroom floor,
But I won't crumble, I'll be more, I will rise again, once more,
The stairs aren't my friends, when my knees disappear,
My back wants to crumble, yeah, this shit is real,
But there are no excuses, I'll always get up again,
"Of course you don't believe me, but have you met me yet?"

"You've got a drug for this, another one for that, but do you have one for me?"
"Or am I just a permanent customer, just something that feeds the machine?"
"You can try to convince me that you're only looking after my needs,"
"But we all really know, you're just another drug pusher on the street."

I make no excuses, I accept all my faults,
I know I'm not useless, stronger than imaginary Gods,
If you need me to prove it, I already have,
Just in case you didn't notice, here I still stand.

There are no excuses, you can never just relent,
You've got to know your purpose, you've got to live your best,
This life can be a circus, can mess you up in the head,
But I know that I'm worth it, "like, have you met me yet?"

First I stumble, then I fall, my face is on the tiled bathroom floor,
But I won't crumble, I'll be more, I will rise again once more,
The stairs aren't my friends when my knees disappear,
My back wants to crumble, yeah, this shit is real,
But there are no excuses, I'll always get up again,
"Of course you don't believe me, but have you met me yet?"

Really, in the end...there are no excuses...,
But, what I've got to ask you...have you met me yet?

23 February, 2025

Solo

Usually, it's my mind that tells my body to move,
But lately there's been a thing, where body wants to choose,
It might be case of, the light shines brightest before it blows,
But even if it is, I'll take advantage of it before it goes.

I would love for someone to come along for the ride with me,
But I know that I have to do this.......solo,
Why would I put someone through what I have to do?
But I know that if they were here, they'd be wonderful,
They would be too wonderful for me,
so I go solo,
and that is the heaviest thing I carry,
Yeah, I know it's a solo journey for me,
I have to do this......solo.

Every day I walk on this Earth, I walk it just to stay alive,
For some this life is just a game, for me it's about survival,
Every single day I walk on this Earth, for me, is all about survival,
For some, this life is just a game, for me, it's about revival,
Of spirit, body and soul, and when I look inside, I know who I can rely on.

I would love for someone to come along for the ride with me,
But I know that I have to do this.......solo,
Why would I put someone through what I have to do,
But I know that if they were here, they'd be wonderful,
They would be too wonderful for me, so I'll just go solo,
Yeah, I know it's a solo journey for me,
I have to do this......solo.

"Hey, Troy. Are you okay? Are you finding it hard to breathe?"
"Well, this breaking body is kinda fucked, but I still have self belief,"
"But that isn't in your realm, we're here about my renal disease,"
"So, let's quit the small talk and discuss the shitshow that is me,"
"Okay, then, we've had a look, and your numbers are really great!"
"You don't need to tell me something I know, have you met me yet?"
"There was no medical change, I just doubled down and worked my arse off,"
"I conditioned myself to lose a lot of weight, remember when I was terminal?"
"This is a game that I know how to play, I don't need any help, I can do it solo,"
"I wake every day, my body's in pain, it's a journey that I can only do on my own."

Usually, it's my mind that tells my body to move,
But lately there's been a thing, where body wants to choose,
It might be case of, the light shines brightest before it blows,
But even if it is, I'll take advantage of it before it goes.

I would love for someone to come along for the ride with me,
But I know that I have to do this.......solo,
Why would I put someone through what I have to do,
But I know that if they were here, they'd be wonderful,
They would be too wonderful for me, so I'll just go solo,
Yeah, I know it's a solo journey for me,
I have to do this......solo.

6 March, 2025

The Hustle

Where's the hustle, where's your fight, don't you want to save your own life,
No time to crumble, no time to die, do anything you have to; to stay alive,
I know I have, I know I've tried, when it comes to fighting, I know this fight,
Yeah, I have to hustle, I am in this fight, it's all part of my plan, just to survive,
There's no losing, no wondering why, I am in this, until the day I die,
I know the hustle, I know the fight, no God saved me, I'm the reason I'm alive.

I have moments when I can't sing, and I feel like I'm living with broken wings,
There are moments when I feel weak, but I will never be one of the meek,
I don't need the Earth, or fancy cars, I just live my life, with my whole damn heart,
I know this life can sometimes be hard, but I've set me sight, for no less than the stars.

"Hey, Troy. Are you okay? Are you finding it hard to breathe?"
"Well, I gotta tell ya, Man. It isn't easy being me,"
"You wouldn't be able to handle it, even if you were at your best,"
"This life of mine might not be easy, but have you met me yet?"

Where's the hustle, where's your fight, don't you want to save your own life,
No time to crumble, no time to die, do anything you have to; to stay alive,
I know I have, I know I've tried, when it comes to fighting, I know this fight,
Yeah, I have to hustle, I am in this fight, it's all part of my plan, just to survive,
There's no losing, no wondering why, I am in this, until the day I die,
I know the hustle, I know the fight, no God saved me, I'm the reason I'm alive.

"You've got a drug for this, a pill for that, do you not see me in front of your face,"
"Are you just blowing a kiss, a magic wish, 'cause I don't have the time to waste,"
"Now come on, Troy. You know why we're here, we're only trying to help,"
"It's kinda funny that you say that to me, but you can save that for someone else."
"You guys told me that I was dying, and I just would not relent"
"I don't know how many times I have to say this, but have you met me yet?"

Now this body, it wants to crumble, it just wants to break down completely,
But I am me, and I know the hustle, and I've got back up, it's called my Beast,
People tell me to take it slower, but I will always refuse to be weak,
They don't know about my hunger, it's how I feed my Beast.

"Hey, Troy. Are you okay? Are you finding it hard to breathe?"
"Well, I gotta tell ya, Man. It isn't easy being me,"
"You wouldn't be able to handle it, even if you were at your best,"
"This life of mine might not be easy, but have you met me yet?"

Where's the hustle, where's your fight, don't you want to save your own life,
No time to crumble, no time to die, do anything you have to; to stay alive,
I know I have, I know I've tried, when it comes to fighting, I know this fight,
Yeah, I have to hustle, I am in this fight, it's all part of my plan, just to survive,
There's no losing, no wondering why, I am in this, until the day I die,
I know the hustle, I know the fight, no God saved me, I'm the reason I'm alive.

Hush now. Hush now, Troy. Don't you dare ever speak,
Hush now. Hush now, Troy. Never admit that your body is weak,
Hush now. Hush now, Troy. Only the stronger side can be seen,
Hush now. Hush now, Troy. "But, I just want to fucking scream!"

"Hey, Troy. Are you okay? Are you finding it hard to breathe?"
"Well, I gotta tell ya, Man. It isn't easy being me,"
"You wouldn't be able to handle it, even if you were at your best,"
"This life of mine might not be easy, but have you met me yet?"

Where's the hustle, where's your fight, don't you want to save your own life,
No time to crumble, no time to die, do anything you have to; to stay alive,
I know I have, I know I've tried, when it comes to fighting, I know this fight,
Yeah, I have to hustle, I am in this fight, it's all part of my plan, just to survive,
There's no losing, no wondering why, I am in this, until the day I die,
I know the hustle, I know the fight, no God saved me, I'm the reason I'm alive.

Hush now. Hush now, Troy. But I can't stop the sound,
The thing about a hush is it's just a scream pushed underground

Yeah, this body of mine wants to break, it's already over 70 percent there,
I hear the crinkles when I stretch my back, it's bubble wrap for the ears,
I laugh it off, even though it hurts, I'm like, 'stupid Troy, did something again',
I know the facts, I'm not stupid like that, but I do get stuck inside my own head,
"So, hush now, Troy. Just relax, it's perfectly fine if you want to rest,"
"I know who you are, you're a counterfeit, you are the God of pretend!"

All of these, imaginary Gods, I know they're just the Demons in my head,
But sometimes it's like, "fuck my life!" Will they ever relent?

But I know the hustle, I know this fight, this is a fight to save my life,
I have my weakness, but I keep it inside, it's the only way I know how to survive,
Don't worry about me, don't even cry,
I've made it this far, and I know exactly why.

12 March, 2025

Complacency

Complacency isn't something I need, I'll always embrace the climb,
Complacency is just the seed of our very own decline,
Complacency is just the disease of the body and mind,
Complacency isn't for me, the work is how I survive.

I'll throw this body of mine, right around the ring,
I am breathing in double time, and I don't feel a thing,
I'm singing a song in my mind, bringing the strength from within,
I am fucking alive, I harden, I fight......and I will win.

I just compartmentalise in my mind the things that don't serve me,
I lock it in a cage and pull down the blinds, so it stops hurting me,
The image is clarified, the confinement feels more psychologically real,
and the active choice to shut out the light carries its own quiet moral weight,
...there's no room for complacency

I will always embrace the climb; the summit is not for me,
Because this life is always a fight, and I just don't do 'easy',
I am the reason that I am alive, there was no God that saved me,
I put in the work with all of my might...
...and there's no room for complacency.

I lift my 15-kilogram dumbbells, as my sweat drips onto the floor,
I am building up this body, just so that I can lift some more,
I don't have time for sorrys, you can just leave them at the door,
And if you think I'll falter, you obviously haven't met me before.

Complacency isn't something I need, I'll always embrace the climb,
Complacency is just the seed of our very own demise,
Complacency is just the disease of the body and mind,
Complacency isn't for me, I work, I fight, I thrive.

Sure, I've been to the brink, and I've looked right over the edge
I like to think of it as the outlook, as I continue to defy my death,
You see, I am a fighter, and I'll keep fighting beyond the bleed,
And I'll always keep on working...
...because there's no time for complacency.

4 April, 2026

Chapter 5:
7 Years Post

T-Shirt Muscles

"Hey, Troy. You're looking good. You look like you're built for speed,"
"Well, I gotta tell ya, Man. It hasn't been fucking easy,"
"What you may perceive as strength is really all illusionary,"
"You see, these are just T-Shirt muscles that hides the weakness in me."

Sure, I've been working out, there are no days off for me,
Sometimes I want to scream and shout, and fuck, I'd love some release,
You know me, I won't ask for help, I just reshape myself into who I need to be,
I've lost heaps of weight, but that's okay, I can manipulate the equation to favour me,
But the problem that I have right now is that there's fuck all more I can lose,
I got myself to under 60 kilograms, and after that, I'm not sure what I'll do,
I can always find a workaround, I can find a cheat better than the best,
But sometimes when I surrender to doubt, I remind myself...."Have you met me yet?"

It's all about the hustle, yeah, it's all about the fight,
There's no time to crumble when you're trying to save your life,
There's no need to be humble, be proud that you have survived,
It's all about your choices, only you can save your life.

Lately, my body hasn't been great, where I'd rather collapse than take the steps I take,
But, I know that's a mistake, my mind needs to be strong, I can't let it break,
If I were to take a moment for myself, I might just....I might just......fall by mistake.

"Hey, Troy. You're looking good. You look like you're built for speed,"
"Well, I gotta tell ya, Man. It hasn't been fucking easy,"
"What you may perceive as strength is really all illusionary,"
"You see, these are just T-Shirt muscles that hides the weakness in me."

I don't like to admit my weakness, but to be honest, I have to be truthful,
What's the point of telling the truth, if it's wrapped in comfort and watered down?
You might think I sound self-indulgent, but I've only had me, to be honest,
Anyone else's help would be a false promise, when it comes down to it...
...T-Shirt muscles don't solve it...

Sure, I've been working out, there are no days off for me,
Sometimes I want to scream and shout, and fuck, I'd love some release,
You know me, I won't ask for help, I just reshape myself into who I need to be,
I've lost heaps of weight, but that's okay, I can manipulate the equation to favour me,
But the problem that I have right now is that there's fuck all more I can lose,
I got myself to under 60 kilograms, and after that, I'm not sure what I'll do,
I can always find a workaround, I can find a cheat better than the best,
But sometimes when I surrender to doubt, I remind myself...."Have you met me yet?"

Now I have times where I feel so weak, but I won't let anyone else see it,
It feels like a crime to just even speak, to say it out loud, is to believe it,
Yeah, I know I'm fucked, but I can't give up, I have a reason to keep being me,
It was never about luck, if it was, I'd be fucked, but I have a reason to believe,
...I have to stay alive, I have to stay alive...
...For my beautiful daughter, Kyra-Lee...

"Hey, Troy. You're looking good. You look like you're built for speed,"
"Well, I gotta tell ya, Man. It hasn't been fucking easy,"
"What you may perceive as strength is really all illusionary,"
"You see, these are just T-Shirt muscles that hides the weakness in me."

And sometimes when I surrender to doubt,
Kyra-Lee's face brings me back yet.

15 March, 2025

Triple Down

I just can't double down anymore, my body doesn't want to comply,
So, instead, I guess I have to triple down and deny the decay inside,
I will always refuse to be pulled down by these Demons that I fight,
Yeah, the time is now to triple down, if I want to stay alive.

It's not just about the quantity of life, it's about quality of life too,
Every day is like black and white, I'd really love some colour too,
This routine that rules my life, I could do with something new,
I know I have earned the right to be alive, but fuck, I'd love to let loose.

This life, it sometimes tries to knock me down...But I get back up again,
This body of mine might be breaking down...But I get back up again,
I know this fight, it likes to bring me down...But I get back up again,
And now it's time for me to triple down...So, I can get back up again.

Now it is time to triple down, double down just won't do,
I'll fight to reclaim my crown, I'll remove this invisible noose,
I will stand and hold my ground, and I will never move,
'Cause when it's time to triple down, double down just won't do.

Sometimes now, when I surrender to doubt, I have to get that out of my head,
I just now have to remind myself..........."Have you met me yet?"
So, without a doubt, I have to triple down, I have to do my best,
And I have no doubt that I can do this now...."Like, have you met me yet?"

This life, it sometimes tries to knock me down...But I get back up again,
This body of mine might be breaking down...But I get back up again,
I know this fight, it likes to bring me down...But I get back up again,
And now it's time for me to triple down...So, I can get back up again.

"You've got a drug for this, another for that, but what does that really mean?"
"You give me a script, and then you punch it out, do you even give a shit about me?"
"Am I just a customer for life, a legal version of buying off the streets?"
"You don't need to explain yourself, I understand, there will always be another me."

And now I have to triple down, double down just won't do,
And now I have to triple down, double down just won't do

It's not just about the quantity of life, it's about quality of life too,
Every day is like black and white, I'd really love some colour too,
This routine that rules my life, I could do with something new,
I know I have earned the right to be alive, but fuck, I'd love to let loose.

This life, it sometimes tries to knock me down...But I get back up again,
This body of mine might be breaking down...But I get back up again,
I know this fight, it likes to bring me down...But I get back up again,
And now it's time for me to triple down...So, I can get back up again.

Yeah, my body is like rice bubbles, snap, crackle, pop,
And I'm still at the table, still eating, and I will not stop.

19 March, 2025

I Don't Want To Die Tonight

I don't want to die tonight, I'm balanced on a knife,
And I've been here before, and I know the weight of this life,
This life has been balanced on a knife, and now I am falling off the side,
I don't want to die tonight, but fuck, I've gotta tell ya, it's been a Hell of a ride.

I have all these Demons in me, they like to lie and tell me I'm not worth it,
They would love me to believe that I will die, without ever having a purpose,
But I see through the shadowed eyes, the ones that hide, I can see the serpent,
I can always spot the spies, the ones that lie, but am I even worth it?

Maybe I'm worth all the judgment, these expectations placed on me,
And when I'm not just up to it, and I am feeling too weak to speak,
Maybe you might comfort me, before I die in my sleep,
I can only hope you will remember me, if only in your dreams.

I don't want to die tonight, I can't crack because I might break,
I just have to find the fight, to make it to tomorrow and the next day,
I don't want to die tonight, but if I have to, I'll do it myself,
I don't want to die tonight, I'll find the fight before the dawn,
I'll always be the one who decides, I've carried this alone too long,
I'll always be the one who decides, I will work it out,
I don't want to die tonight, but if I have to die..............

..There's only one question left............. "Have you met me yet?"
........"Like, really, have you met me yet?"

I don't die, I don't quit, I will live to the end of my existence,
When my time comes around, I will meet it with full resistance,
I am a fighter, I'm one of the best, only because I know this fight,
So, when it comes down to it.....I'll see you tomorrow,
........in the morning light.

I don't want to die tonight, I can't crack because I might break,
I just have to find the fight, to make it to tomorrow and the next day,
I don't want to die tonight, but if I have to, I'll do it myself,
This is not a suicide rhyme, nor is it an ask for help,
I'll always be the one who decides, I will work it out,
I don't want to die tonight, but if I have to die...............

I don't want to die tonight, and I'll fight it with full resistance,
But sometimes this fight, it just steals my life, and I just want to give in,
Sympathy was never my weapon of choice,
I had to find the Beast inside,
The one that sharpened silence into something I could use,
I had to find the Beast inside, my killer, the one that doesn't deceive me.

I have all these Demons in me, they like to lie and tell me I'm not worth it,
They would love me to believe that I will die, without ever having a purpose,
But I see through the shadowed eyes, the ones that hide, I can see the serpent,
I can always spot the spies, the ones that lie, but am I even worth it?

I don't want to die tonight, I can't crack because I might break,
I just have to find the fight, to make it to tomorrow and the next day,
I don't want to die tonight, but if I have to, I'll do it myself,
This is not a suicide rhyme, nor is it an ask for help,
I'll always be the one who decides, I will work it out,
I don't want to die tonight, but if I have to die...............

I don't want to die tonight, but nothing is set in concrete,
Even though my body conspires to make me feel weak,
I will always try to fight and stand on my own two feet,
Because I know that I can't rely on anyone being there for me,
Yeah, I know it's of my own doing, I just push people away,
I don't want to be someone's burden, there's no need to pray,
If I make it, I make it, but if I don't, that's completely okay,
I don't want to die tonight, but if I do, there's really nothing left to say.

There's other things happening in my life, more than my body breaking down,
And sometimes I just want to close my eyes, and possibly reach out,
But, then again, I could never do that, 'cause I'm the one who has to do for himself,
I close my eyes and wish I could reach out,
But I have always been the saddest clown,
The one who laughs the loudest on his way down

It's not your problem, it's not your burden, sympathy was never for me,
Down strange corridors, drowning in purgatory, I'm kinda stuck in the in between,
But I'm defiant, I still believe, I am completely contradictory,
So, I won't die, I'll stay here, even though my body is fucking up on me,

I don't want to die tonight, I can't crack because I might break,
I just have to find the fight, to make it to tomorrow and the next day,
I don't want to die tonight, but if I have to, I'll do it myself,
This is not a suicide rhyme, nor is it an ask for help,
I'll always be the one who decides, I will work it out.
I don't want to die tonight, but if I have to die...............

I don't want to lie tonight, I'm really not doing that great,
I don't want to cry tonight, because that would only be my selfish self,
I don't want to lie tonight, but I'm only lying to myself,
I don't want to die tonight, I don't want to die tonight.

I'm sorry that I didn't ask for your help..........

29 March, 2025

Rice Bubbles

Now my body is like Rice Bubbles, there's always a snap, crackle and pop,
Maybe I should ask for a sponsorship from the breakfast cereal company, Kellogg's,
But now, on a serious note, you wouldn't want to be in my skin,
Sometimes it is hard to even hope, in this skinbag full of broken bits,
Now I am not complaining, I face all of my challenges head-on,
It's just getting a little harder now, there's always a snap, crackle and pop.

And while this might be restricting, I have to keep on moving,
I refuse to be the victim, even though my body is unforgiving,
I am not a sucker for pain, I just know it very well,
To some, it might be just a game, but to me, it is fucking Hell.

Even with my restrictions, I'll never lack conviction,
This can be my religion, one where I am forgiven,
I can beat the system, it's something that I've lived in,
I don't need forgiveness, 'cause I'm the guy that doesn't give in.

I'm the guy that doesn't give in……
I'm the guy that doesn't give in……
I'm the guy that doesn't give in…….
I am still breathin', I am still livin'.

Now my body is like Rice Bubbles, there's always a snap, crackle and pop,
Maybe I should ask for a sponsorship from the breakfast cereal company, Kellogg's,
But now, on a serious note, you wouldn't want to be in my skin,
Sometimes it is hard to even hope, in this skinbag full of broken bits,
Now I am not complaining, I face all of my challenges head-on,
It's just getting a little harder now, there's always a snap, crackle and pop.

"Hey, Troy. Are you okay? Are you finding it hard to breathe?"
"Well, to be honest with you, there are days that bring me to my knees,"
"But it's okay, it's all alright, I live each day like I've won a million-dollar bet,"
"Because after all, you should know by now, like, have you met me yet?"

I've been at the edge, I've been to the brink, but I prefer to think of it as the outlook instead,
It's not how I feel, it's about how I choose to think, it's not about no, it's about yes.

And while this might be restricting, I have to keep on moving,
I refuse to be the victim, even though my body is unforgiving,
I am not a sucker for pain, I just know it very well,
To some, it might be just a game, but to me, it is fucking Hell.

Now my body is like Rice Bubbles, there's always a snap, crackle and pop,
Maybe I should ask for a sponsorship from the breakfast cereal company, Kellogg's,
But now, on a serious note, you wouldn't want to be in my skin,
Sometimes it is hard to even hope, in this skinbag full of broken bits,
Now I am not complaining, I face all of my challenges head-on,
It's just getting a little harder now, there's always a snap, crackle and pop.

It's not about no, it's all about yes

2 April, 2025

Strength

"C'mon, have you even met me yet? You should know by now that I don't relent,"
"These last twelve months have been a bet. One that you thought I wouldn't get,"
"Hey, Troy. Are you okay? Are you finding it hard to breathe?"
"C'mon, now. This doesn't need to be a sermon, you just need to listen to me."

I've been cutting, but not in the way you might think,
I've been dropping, dropping weight like unneeded bricks,
I have been training to convince my body that it needs me,
I have been trying, trying so hard to change my own reality,
When it comes to eating, I don't really do much of that now,
And it's probably a good thing, 'cause I can't afford it anyhow.

Yeah, this cost-of-living crisis is a bitch, I know I'm not alone, we all feel it,
But, when it takes sixty per cent of my pension, just to pay the rent, and keep living.....
There's not a lot left over. Can I pay my internet? What happens if I'm late with my rent?
There's all these balls in the air, and I'm not a juggler, it kinda makes it hard to handle it.

Strength is my answer, strength will be saviour, I'll save myself, at the twelfth hour,
Now I'll get stronger, procrastinating no longer, I don't need help, I know my own power,
I was cutting, but now it's time to get bigger, my Beast needs feeding, and I'll feed it,
Because strength is my King, I won a million-dollar bet, I've done 10 workouts today,

...............is that enough yet?
...............is that enough yet?

I've switched up from my 12.5-kilo dumbbells to the 15-kilo variety,
And yeah, I know I've gotta take it slow, but taking it slow doesn't keep me alive,
I don't know what my timeframe is, but make no mistake, the clock is ticking,
"But, hey, guess what? In a couple of weeks, this guy will be 55, and still living."

My plan for the next twelve months is to get stronger and build my strength,
I will build this body, I will take it to its limits, I will build a better me,
I don't care about the pain, it's not an excuse not to move,
Because if I let it bother me, it would only weaken me...

Strength is my answer, strength will be saviour, I'll save myself, at the twelfth hour,
Now I'll get stronger, procrastinating no longer, I don't need help, I know my own power,
I was cutting, but now it's time to get bigger, my Beast needs feeding, and I'll feed it,
Because strength is my King, I won a million-dollar bet, I've done 10 workouts today,
...............is that enough yet?
...............is that enough yet?

Even though my back is breaking, and my knees want to complain,
My shoulders might be aching, but I refuse to give it a name,
My pain is my power, that's where my Beast comes into the game,
He is my saviour, he is my strength, and we share the same name……

I've been cutting, but not in the way you might think,
I've been dropping, dropping weight like unneeded bricks,
I have been training to convince my body that it needs me,
I have been trying, trying so hard to change my own reality,
When it comes to eating, I don't really do much of that now.
And it's probably a good thing, 'cause I can't afford it anyhow

"Hey, Troy. We have some news for you, it's not something that you want to hear,"
"But, we found something that needs a discussion, it's probably best you have a seat,"
"You know that I don't sit, it hurts my back, if you want to talk to me, I will just stand,"
"Well, now, Troy. We've found something that we've graded at a 3,"
"There's nothing to worry about right now, we've booked you in on the 16th."

That's a story for another day, no one needs to get down on their knees and pray,
I know my body, I know my brain, I know my emotional state,
I know what I need to do, I have to work harder than ever before,
I have to triple down, double down won't do no more.

Strength is my answer, strength will be saviour, I'll save myself, at the twelfth hour,
Now I'll get stronger, procrastinating no longer, I don't need help, I know my own power,
I was cutting, but now it's time to get bigger, my Beast needs feeding, and I'll feed it,
Because strength is my King, I won a million-dollar bet, I've done 10 workouts today.
................is that enough yet?
................is that enough yet?

"Hey, Troy. Are you okay? Are you finding it hard to breathe?"
"What the actual fuck? You already know that I'm a ticking time machine,"
"But your clock don't matter to me, I can find the strength in me."
"Something that you might not know about me...............
.............I am a completely different kind of Beast,"

And I know the strength that I have in me.

4 April, 2025

No Ceilings Here

There are no ceilings here, there's no limits left,
I can look up to the sky, feeling like I won a million-dollar bet,
I still have belief in me, and I will never relent,
For those of you who doubted me, "Have you met me yet?"

You can't put this dog down, you can't kill me dead,
I am still defiant, "like, have you met me yet?"
If you want to try me, you will lose the bet,
"You say that I am dying, but have you met me yet?"

"Move more so you can move more", it's one of the things I tell myself,
Do more so you can do more, it's the only way I can work it out,
Movement is my medicine, it's my King without a crown,
My Beast defeats my enemies, that's why I'm alive now.

"Hey, Troy. Are you okay? Are you finding it hard to breathe?"
"Nah, Mate. I'm completely golden. I'm the ruler of my disease,"
This body of mine might be breaking, but you won't see me on my knees,
So, you can forget the hating, it's of no use to me,
I'm living each day like I won a million-dollar bet,
I'm the living proof, "like, have you met me yet?"

There are no ceilings here, there's no limits left,
I can look up to the sky, feeling like I won a million-dollar bet,
I still have belief in me, and I will never relent,
For those of you who doubted me, "have you met me yet?"

I ain't dying, I'm a fighter, I am in it all the way,
No use trying, if you give up fighting, I know how to play this game,
Internal sirens, set off like lightning, throbbing through my veins,
My mind needs quieting, overthinking me, I am golden, just the same.

Breaking down, breaking down, breaking down on me,
Breaking down, breaking down, breaking down on me,
Breaking down, breaking down, breaking down on me,
Breaking down, breaking down....but I'll rise again, you'll see.

You can't put this dog down, you can't kill me dead,
I am still defiant, "like, have you met me yet?"
If you want to try me, you will lose the bet,
"You say that I am dying, but have you met me yet?"

There are no ceilings here, there's no limits left,
I can look up to the sky, feeling like I won a million-dollar bet,
I still have belief in me, and I will never relent,
For those of you who doubted me, "Have you met me yet?"

My right knee is gone, and my back is a disgrace,
But you won't ever see it expressed on my face,
The weakness that lives in me is not for public consumption,
"Oh, I'm sorry, were you busy? I'm sorry for the interruption."

And yes, there are ceilings here, I built them myself,
Then smashed straight through. No limits left.

10 April, 2025

7 Years Post

Now I'm coming up to 7 years post transplant, my, how time can fly,
It's like I've learned a different language, all in the blink of an eye,
"Here you go, Troy. Have a tuna sandwich". The nurses said to me three times a week,
When I was in the dialysis chair, watching the blood go in and out of me,
Not too long after that, I had graduated to an at-home dialysis machine,
I had to plug myself in when I went to bed, and be careful not to turn in my sleep,
And I had to have an extra-long extension cord, in case, in the night, I needed a leak,
And now I'm coming up to 7 years post-transplant, because I killed my weak.

I remember it all with such clarity, the struggle, the fight, the biggest of my life,
Sometimes it just felt like insanity, the crumble, don't cry, just dry my eyes,
Yet, I still face everyday, exactly like I've won a million-dollar bet,
"Yeah, I know you've heard it all before, but have you met me yet?"

There are more challenges that will come my way,
And I will always handle it, I'm here to save my day,
The only Hero in this story is my donor and his gift,
I just try to fight the good fight, all in honour of him.

On 26 June, in this year of twenty twenty five,
It will be 7 years post-transplant, and I am still alive!
"Man, it's been a trip! All these lows and all the highs,"
I just completely went off script, just so I could survive,
I had to do this my own way, just to keep myself alive,
I always had my Beast with me, standing side by side.

Now I'm coming up to 7 years post transplant, my, how time can fly,
It's like I've learned a different language, all in the blink of an eye,
"Here you go, Troy. Have a tuna sandwich". The nurses said to me three times a week,
When I was in the dialysis chair, watching the blood go in and out of me,
Not too long after that, I had graduated to an at-home dialysis machine,
I had to plug myself in when I went to bed, and be careful not to turn in my sleep,
And I had to have an extra-long extension cord, in case, in the night, I needed a leak,
And now I'm coming up to 7 years post-transplant, because I killed my weak.

I know I'm jumping ahead, and there's still a couple of months to go,
But I don't deal with the negative, because it fucks with my flow,
And like you'll see, in a future write that has yet to be,
It's time for me to celebrate, it's time for me to celebrate me,
Acknowledge what I've done, everything that I have achieved,
Me and my donor, hand in hand, we will both succeed.

There are more challenges that will come my way,
And I will always handle it, I'm here to save my day,
The only Hero in this story is my donor and his gift,
I just try to fight the good fight, all in honour of him.

Now I'm coming up to 7 years post transplant, my, how time can fly,
It's like I've learned a different language, all in the blink of an eye,
"Here you go, Troy. Have a tuna sandwich". The nurses said to me three times a week,
When I was in the dialysis chair, watching the blood go in and out of me,
Not too long after that, I had graduated to an at-home dialysis machine,
I had to plug myself in when I went to bed, and be careful not to turn in my sleep,
And I had to have an extra-long extension cord, in case, in the night, I needed a leak,
And now I'm coming up to 7 years post-transplant, because I killed my weak.

"Hey, Troy. Are you okay? Are you finding it hard to breathe?"
"Nah, Mate. I'll be alright. You have seen the fight in me"

20 April, 2025

55

On Wednesday, just last week, I made it to the dinosaur age of 55,
I don't really care that I'm prehistoric, I am just happy to still be alive,
And now it's time to celebrate me, I'm going to celebrate my entire life,
Terminal now feels like a distant memory, now that I made it to 55.

"Hey, Troy. Happy Birthday! We hope that you had a wonderful day,"
"Hey there, thanks for saying. It's one that will remain in my memories always,"
"It was just a chilled-out day, with the people that are most important to me,"
"I spent the day with my lovely Mother and my wonderful daughter, Kyra-Lee."

I got all my workouts in, first thing in the morning,
I had to get my steps all done before anyone came calling,
I did all this, as well as a couple of bonus things,
And when it came to celebrate, bourbon was my drink.

On Wednesday, just last week, I made it to the dinosaur age of 55,
I don't really care that I'm prehistoric, I am just happy to still be alive,
And now it's time to celebrate me, I'm going to celebrate my entire life,
Terminal now feels like a distant memory, now that I made it to 55.

I was 48 years of age when I got my life-saving donation,
But when I was only 46 years of age, I was told there was no saving me,
I just sat down and thought to myself, these guys are bloody crazy,
"After all, have you met me yet?" I've got no room for maybe's.

Now we're getting close to 7 years post, it's just a couple of months away,
This kidney donation I host, oh, my donor's ghost, I am defying the grave,
My back might be breaking, but I ain't complaining, I always kill my weak,
At risk of overtraining, but that's the route I'm taking, I just do what works for me.

"Hey, Troy. Happy Birthday! We hope that you had a wonderful day,"
"Hey there, thanks for saying. It's one that will remain in my memories always,"
"It was just a chilled-out day, with the people that are most important to me,"
"I spent the day with my lovely Mother and my wonderful daughter, Kyra-Lee."

On Wednesday, just last week, I made it to the dinosaur age of 55,
I don't really care that I'm prehistoric, I am just happy to still be alive,
And now it's time to celebrate me, I'm going to celebrate my entire life,
Terminal now feels like a distant memory, now that I made it to 55.

Yeah, I've made it to 55, and there were those who doubted my fight,
Well, here I am, I'm still alive........in the garden of adversity, I'll always thrive.

20 April, 2025

Celebrate Me

Here I am now, I'm exactly where I'm supposed to be,
It's time for me to acknowledge everything that I have achieved,
I have always just refused to live my life on my knees,
Yeah, it's time for me to celebrate; it's time for me to celebrate me.

I have worked my arse off, there's absolutely no doubt about that,
I am not shackled now, but there's still no time for me to relax,
I can turn my eyes backwards and look at all the work I've done,
But now I'm looking outwards, and my future has just begun.

I will always put in the work, it is just the way that I am built,
Ignore the pain, ignore the hurt, keep improving my skills,
You can fill that hole in the dirt, I just can't be killed,
Make that call, cancel the hearse, all I need is my will.

Here I am now, I'm exactly where I'm supposed to be,
It's time for me to acknowledge everything that I have achieved,
I have always just refused to live my life on my knees,
Yeah, it's time for me to celebrate; it's time for me to celebrate me.

I will take a moment......just to breathe,
I will take a moment......just for me,
I will take a moment......and just release,
I will take a moment......to celebrate me.

I've earned my pause, I've earned my right to rest,
Sure, I could do that if I want to end up dead,
"Hey, what's the time? Is it time to work out again?"
Who am I kidding? There are no days off for me left.

'Home Sweet Home', that's the only place for me,
Tommy Lee did it best when he played it on the keys,
Where's my 'Dr. Feelgood?', "Nah, kidding. That's not for me,"
"But fuck, I've gotta tell ya, I've earned the right to celebrate me."

"Hey, Troy. How are you going? I've seen you a lot lately,"
"You know me, I'm proactive. My health is my priority,"
"If I find a problem, I can't ignore it. I'm just trying to stay healthy,"
"Okay, I've got it. We will do all the tests you need."

Here I am now, I'm exactly where I'm supposed to be,
It's time for me to acknowledge everything that I have achieved,
I have always just refused to live my life on my knees,
Yeah, it's time for me to celebrate; it's time for me to celebrate me.

I will take a moment......just to breathe,
I will take a moment......just for me,
I will take a moment......and just release,
I will take a moment......to celebrate me.

Here I am now, I'm exactly where I'm supposed to be.
It's time for me to acknowledge everything that I have achieved.
I have always just refused to live my life on my knees.
Yeah, it's time for me to celebrate; it's time for me to celebrate me.

I will take a moment, just a moment.....to celebrate me

20 April, 2025

Inspiration

"Hey, Chris. Are you okay? Are you finding it hard to breathe?"
Yep, you guessed it, this is about inspiration, it's not about me,
It's about a bloke, who's wife followed my Facebook feed,
I used to post my steps daily, and it gave him some self-belief,
I didn't know about it at the time that he had found inspiration in me,
But while I was inspiring him, he was inspiring me……
…………maybe we could both succeed.

I'm very sad to say that he didn't make it to today,
The thing that did him in was his very last hospital stay,
"We're really sorry to say, your Husband's got a hospital infection,"
"We really did try our very best, but we just couldn't help him."

You see, Chris was like me, both suffering from renal disease,
And when he saw my conviction, he said to his wife, Alli,
"If he can do it, so can I! I don't have to give in at all!"
And it bought him another year or two,
More mornings, more light,
Before the quiet came.

Inspiration can come from anywhere, as simple as a daily fb post,
To show your improvement, to show how you have grown,
If I can do it, and Chris can do it, you can do it too,
It's never a competition, we just all want to improve,
We don't all get to win the race, we know there's an end,
Just don't fall, live with grace, and I'll see you again....my friend.

I like to think that before Chris left, he went with a smile, without an ounce of regret,
So, for Chris and others like us, we've got five words for you: "Have you met us yet?"

"Hey, Chris. Are you okay? Are you finding it hard to breathe?"
Yep, you guessed it, this is about inspiration, it's not about me,
It's about a bloke, who's wife followed my Facebook feed,
I used to post my steps daily, and it gave him some self-belief,
I didn't know about it at the time that he had found inspiration in me,
But while I was inspiring him, he was inspiring me......
............maybe we could both succeed.

Just stand strong..........and you can hold on,
Just stand strong..........it's here that you belong,
Just stand strong..........sing your own damn song,
Just stand strong..........just stand strong.

Inspiration can come from anywhere, as simple as a daily fb post,
To show your improvement, to show how you have grown,
If I can do it, and Chris can do it, you can do it too,
It's never a competition, we just all want to improve,
We don't all get to win the race, we know there's an end,
Just don't fall, live with grace, and I'll see you again....my friend.

"Hey, Chris. Are you okay? Are you finding it hard to breathe?"
Yep, you guessed it, this is about inspiration, it's not about me,
It's about a bloke, who's wife followed my Facebook feed,
I used to post my steps daily, and it gave him some self-belief,
I didn't know about it at the time that he had found inspiration in me,
But while I was inspiring him, he was inspiring me......
............maybe we could both succeed.

So, I will raise my glass and give a cheers to you,
Chris, my lost compadre, I take inspiration from you.

26 April, 2025

153

Chapter 6:
26 June, 2025

The Garden Of Adversity

In the garden of adversity, I will always thrive,
I am the weed that nobody wanted, and the seed that bloomed anyway,
I am the cockroach and the empath, and I thrive the very same way,
In the garden of adversity, is where I am alive,
I was weak, then found strength, on the inside,
In the garden of adversity, I will always thrive.

You can't keep me down, no matter what you throw at me,
I have seen through the clouds, right into my clarity,
For a while there, I thought it was all insanity,
But I've been around, and now I thrive in adversity.

"Hey, Troy. Are you okay? Are you finding it hard to breathe?"
"C.mon, Mate. I've been down before, but I rise above adversity,"
"You've seen me thrive, and stay alive, I'll always defy my death,"
"Do I even have to say it? Like, have you met me yet?"

The heavier weights are getting more comfortable,
When I go back to the lesser weights, I feel unstoppable,
Like gravity has learned to give,
In this garden of adversity that I live.

In the garden of adversity, I will always thrive,
I am the weed, I am the cockroach, that refuses to die,
In the garden of adversity, you will see me smile,
I am the seed, I am empathy, and I will always shine,
In the garden of adversity, is where I am alive,
I was weak, then found strength, on the inside,
In the garden of adversity, I will always thrive.

I will fight, I will fight, I will fight for my life,
It's what I've done from my birth until tonight,
I won't cry, I won't cry, I'm totally alright,
In the garden of adversity is where I thrive.

You can't keep me down, no matter what you throw at me,
I have seen through the clouds, right into my clarity,
For a while there, I thought it was all insanity,
But I've been around, and now I thrive in adversity.

In the garden of adversity, I will always thrive,
I am the weed, I am the cockroach, that refuses to die,
In the garden of adversity, you will see me smile,
I am the seed, I am empathy, and I will always shine,
In the garden of adversity, is where I am alive,
I was weak, then found strength, on the inside,
In the garden of adversity, I will always thrive.

For Mary, and for Chris, and all those going through pain,
I will carry my burden of bliss and live to make it another day.

In the garden of adversity, I do thrive,
Do anything you have to, just to stay alive,
Remember those before you, the ones that died,
Take it as inspiration to keep yourself alive.

26 April, 2025

Does It Even Need To Be Said?

Well, I guess it must be close to the time to ease up on these writes,
I will still continue to express my mind, just in different styles,
I will still come back and visit here, after all, it's kinda the story of my life,
These last nine years, where I adapted, I fought, and I survived!

Yeah, I know you've heard it all before, about Troy and how he'll soar,
About how he struggled and how he fought, sometimes, maybe, less is more,
But, at least I'm alive and made it to today, and I did it all my own way,
I survived the greatest escape, and I can always fix my own mistakes.

"Hey, Troy. How are you today? You've been doing really well lately,"
"Yeah, well, I had to triple down. Double down wasn't doing enough for me,"
"Your numbers are looking really good, you really know what you are doing,"
"Well, when you've been terminal like me, it's live, or be buried in ruins."

In the garden of adversity, I will always thrive,
It's like a personal University, one that's about my life,
There's no point calling the hearse for me, I will always fight,
You can think better or worse of me, but I'll do what I have to…..to survive.

It's almost like I'm now Troy 3.0, I've upgraded to sustain the fight,
In my story, I'm my only Hero, it's only me who can save my life.

"Hey, Troy. How are you today? You've been doing really well lately,"
"Yeah, well, I had to triple down. Double down wasn't doing enough for me,"
"Your numbers are looking really good, you really know what you are doing,"
"Well, when you've been terminal like me, it's live, or be buried in ruins."

Well, I guess it must be close to the time to ease up on these writes,
I will still continue to express my mind, just in different styles,
I will still come back and visit here, after all, it's kinda the story of my life,
These last nine years, where I adapted, I fought, and I survived!

"Hey, Troy. How are you today? You've been doing really well lately,"
"Yeah, well, I had to triple down. Double down wasn't doing enough for me,"
"Your numbers are looking really good, you really know what you are doing,"
"Well, when you've been terminal like me, it's live, or be buried in ruins."

Does it even need to be said, "like, have you even met me yet?

6 May, 2025

The Necessary Guy

I've always been the necessary guy,
The one you call when things turn to shit,
Now I struggle to be the relevant guy,
What the fuck happened to all those years?
Now I'm just the lonely guy,
All because I'm immunosuppressed,
So, now I have to be the necessary guy,
Not for you, but for me instead.

I have to focus all of my energy, on me, myself and I,
This condition isn't temporary, this is for the rest of my life,
I have to do what's necessary, if I want to stay alive,
And I will do everything, I'll kick, I'll bite, I'll fight.

It can sometimes be a lonely existence,
When everything is planned around my meds,
And you can forget about a social life,
Those days have long been spent,
But when it comes to me, I'll go the distance,
Really, "like, have you met me yet?"
So, for me, this fight is never over,
Let's face it; it's better than being dead.

"Hey, Troy. Are you busy? Can you lend a hand?"
"I'd really love to help you out, but I've already got plans,"
"Oh, Troy. Why won't you help? You can do your stuff later,"
"Yeah, well, I'll tell ya, Man. I've got a strict timetable,"
"So, this time, you'll have to help yourself, sometimes I'm not able,"
"And if you can't understand that....then maybe I'll see you later."

I've always been the necessary guy,
The one you call when things turn to shit,
Now I struggle to be the relevant guy,
What the fuck happened to all those years?
Now I'm just the lonely guy.
All because I'm immunosuppressed,
So, now I have to be the necessary guy,
Not for you, but for me instead.

I have to focus all of my energy on me, myself and I,
This condition isn't temporary, this is for the rest of my life,
I have to do what's necessary if I want to stay alive,
And I will do everything, I'll kick, I'll bite, I'll fight.

I used to be the necessary guy,
Now sometimes, I'm not able,
How can I be the relevant guy,
Now that time has turned the tables.

I've always been the necessary guy,
The one you call when things turn to shit,
Now I struggle to be the relevant guy,
What the fuck happened to all those years?
Now I'm just the lonely guy,
All because I'm immunosuppressed,
So, now I have to be the necessary guy,
Not for you, but for me instead.

I used to be the necessary guy,
Now I'm not even the relevant guy,
My, it's funny how time can remake a man,
And now that time has turned the tables.

I've always been the necessary guy,
The one you call when things turn to shit,
Now I struggle to be the relevant guy,
What the fuck happened to all those years?
Now I'm just the lonely guy,
All because I'm immunosuppressed,
So, now I have to be the necessary guy,
Not for you, but for me instead.

6 May, 2025

Third Gear

"Hey, Troy. Are you okay? Are you finding it hard to breathe?"
"It's funny that you ask me that, because I'm trying to be a fitter me,"
"Oh, really? You already do too much, don't you have any fear?"
"Nah, Mate. I'm alright, I'm not even in third gear!"

I'll push, and I'll push, and I'll push some more,
This is my fight, it's my own personal war,
I'll rise, and I'll rise, and I'll rise, until I soar,
This life that I have is worth fighting for.

I refuse to give my pain a name, I prefer to call it awareness,
I have a Beast that can't be tamed, he handles my defences,
All my chips are in this game, it's no wonder that I'm restless,
And I will win either way, I'm immune to the temptress.

I know that I said that I would ease up on these writes,
But there's stuff in my head that needs releasing tonight,
I've written a couple others, not from this collection,
Just to try to distract myself and go in another direction,
I can tell you about 'White Flag', or 'The Champions Of Yesterday,'
But it's within these writes that I have something to say.

"Hey, Troy. Are you okay? Are you finding it hard to breathe?"
"It's funny that you ask me that, because I'm trying to be a fitter me,"
"Oh, really? You already do too much, don't you have any fear?"
"Nah, Mate. I'm alright, I'm not even in third gear!"

Today I went to see an Exercise Physiologist,
Looking for practicalities, not empty promises,
Yeah, I'm a sceptic, I'm used to doing things my own way,
But, I've gotta say it's tempting to once again engage,
Being immunosuppressed, it's not an easy game,
But maybe I'll dip my toe in, just to feel some change.

I've made an appointment, just to view the site,
Just to gauge, even remotely, if it's something to try,
I really need something different, I hope it feels right,
But it's alright if it isn't, I'll always get by.

Fourth gear is not yet in my sight, but it's always just around the corner ,
It's a good thing I know this fight, because I can always work harder,
I know the young people say "fuck my life", but it's about being smarter,
I know all about dancing on a knife, and I wish to fuck it didn't matter.

I'll push, and I'll push, and I'll push some more,
This is my fight, it's my own personal war,
I'll rise, and I'll rise, and I'll rise, until I soar,
This life that I have is worth fighting for.

"Hey, Troy. Are you okay? Are you finding it hard to breathe?"
"It's funny that you ask me that, because I'm trying to be a fitter me,"
"Oh, really? You already do too much, don't you have any fear?"
"Nah, Mate. I'm alright, I'm not even in third gear!"

All of this series is for me, it's about teaching myself about my own life,
And you can have it for free, there's no conditional trial,
Just remember when things are bleakest, you can still smile,
Laughter is the best medicine, by a Goddamn country mile!

I'll push, and I'll push, and I'll push some more,
This is my fight, it's my own personal war,
I'll rise, and I'll rise, and I'll rise, until I soar,
This life that I have is worth fighting for.

We know about this series, and the title that I present,
"You should know better, my friend. Because we have definitely met."

9 May, 2025

26 June, 2025

On this 26th day of June, in this year of 2025,
I am very happy to say that I am still alive,
It's been seven years post, and I am living my life,
And I get to say that......... with a great big smile.

Sure, it's been tricky, and I've had to pick my fights,
Sometimes I've been unlucky, when I didn't get it right,
But that's the beauty of living, you get to go again,
As if you didn't know it, "like, have you met me yet?"

Now it's seven years today, and I still defy the grave,
Mr. Reaper's gone away, it's a game he couldn't play,
And I am very happy to say that I am still alive today,
And I did it all my own way, so hip-hip-hooray!

On 13 June, just nine short years ago,
And I did it all my own way, 7 years post today,
Oh, you had to blue line going to the line,
I looked back at them and slowly shook my head,
Whilst thinking to myself, "Have you met me yet?"

Cursed with a Conscience

I'm cursed with a conscience, it's just not my choice to choose,
If I am witness to a problem, I just have to interlude,
It's not like that I want to, I must have on my morality shoes,
I'm cursed with a conscience, and I wish I could be more like you.

Sometimes I wish I could just close my eyes and pretend that I don't see,
But I just can't, I just can't deny, that just would not be me,
I am simply cursed with a conscience, I guess I have morality,
I just can't ignore the world's problems, and somebody has to speak.

I can't see anyone else raising their hand, so I guess it's up to me,
And when it is only one man, it is so hard for the world to see,
We could make a chorus as a crowd, together, you and me,
We can make a stand and make it right now, if only you believed.

I'm cursed with a conscience, I wish I could be more like you,
But, I guess that just isn't me, my blindfold I have removed,
I know that we all have problems when we can feel the noose,
But I just can't close my eyes, it's not a choice I get to choose.

I'm cursed with a conscience, why can't I be more like you,
Now I have this responsibility that I just cannot remove,
I am only one single man, but what about you,
Do you feel the weight of all the damage you've refused?

I can feel a heart breaking, from right across the room,
I am cursed with a conscience, but I have empathy too,
I just can't ignore the simple things that people refuse to do,
If I see a dollar drop from your pocket, I'll give it back to you.

I'm cursed with a conscience, but fuck, I wish I wasn't,
If I don't do the right thing, it will always haunt me,
Why do I feel alone in this? Isn't this all of our responsibility?
I'm cursed with a conscience, and I guess that's just my problem.

4 April, 2026

7 Years Post

I don't give in, I don't die, I will fight for my life,
I will win, it's my right, I am fire, I always survive.

I will walk with purpose, I will lengthen my stride,
I'll keep my head above the surface of this rising tide,
You'll see a resurgence, it's right there in my eyes,
Yeah, this fight is worth it; it is my time to shine.

Now it's seven years today, and I still defy the grave,
Mr. Reaper's gone away, it's a game he couldn't play,
And I am very happy to say that I am still alive today,
And I did it all my own way, so hip-hip-hooray!

"Hey, Troy. Don't you know that you're going to die?"
"In fact, we're all amazed that you're still alive,"
"You see, you're down to just 1% of kidney functionality,"
"Hey, Troy. Are you okay? Are you finding it hard to breathe?"

"Nah, Mate. I'm alright. I've got lots of fight left,"
"You tell me that I'm dying, but have you met me yet?"
"You see, there's something about me that you don't know,"
"I've been a fighter from birth, and I can still take all of these blows."

On this 26th day of June, in this year of 2025,
I am very happy to say that I am still alive,
It's been seven years post, and I am living my life,
And I get to say that......... with a great big smile.

It's a dance between two strangers, in such a primal way,
This cowardly disease, that thought that I could break,
It put me on my knees, but I knew that I would rise again,
And here I am, you see, I'm standing here today.

Now it's seven years today, and I still defy the grave,
Mr. Reaper's gone away, it's a game he couldn't play,
And I am very happy to say that I am still alive today,
And I did it all my own way, so hip-hip-hooray!

I've been doing this for more than a minute, and I've got it right more than wrong,
Sometimes I've felt like I should be committed, but I sang my own damn song,
This is a fight that is worth winning, and I've known it all along,
I am not one to just give in, it's my Beast that makes me strong.

My strength always came from within, it never came from without,
If this is a game, I'm in it to win it, of that you can have no doubt,
I never cared about evil or sin, I just knew I had to help myself,
And I've shown that I don't give in, that's why I'm still standing now.

Now I'm going to the gym, on every Friday morning,
It's just an add-on to everything else that I'm doing,
I'm trying to be superfit, increasing all my training,
And I'll give Death a kiss and a smile as I'm waving,
Goodbye to Mr Reaper, maybe I'll see you later,
I guess you lost this game of scissors, rock and paper,
I don't need no help, I am my own saviour,
Goodbye, Mr Reaper, I won't be seeing you later.

Now it's seven years today, and I still defy the grave,
Mr. Reaper's gone away, it's a game he couldn't play,
And I am very happy to say that I am still alive today,
And I did it all my own way, so hip-hip-hooray!

Just a couple weeks ago, I went for another biopsy,
You see, I'd received a grading of 3 as a precursor for the Big C.

The funny thing about it, it was my anniversary,
It was nine years to the day, they told me I was terminal,
But I got my results straight after my procedure,
And I'm still standing strong, there's no cancer in me,
But I still have a precursor, in the higher range,
Thanks to my meds, that kill me while they save,
Throw all you got at me, 'cause I'm a true believer,
I'll always beat the odds. How can I be clearer?

It's my second dance, with this stranger known as cancer,
But when it comes to me......I am the danger,
And sometimes I want to forget, and wish I had....amnesia,
This fight is kinda tough........sometimes I feel like I've had enough,
Sometimes I feel like I've had enough.......
But, I have to be strong enough.....I will be strong enough,
So, I'll be waving to you when I see ya later......

Now it's seven years today, and I still defy the grave,
Mr. Reaper's gone away, it's a game he couldn't play,
And I am very happy to say that I am still alive today,
And I did it all my own way, so hip-hip-hooray!

Yeah, I'm doing great, and I'm doing it all without a court subpoena,
But I still have to work harder, with the return of osteopenia,
It's not all that bad, really, it's only in both of my femurs,
So, I'm gonna crack the whip again and walk towards my future.

I don't give in, I don't die, this is a fight for my life,
I'm no quitter, I'll always strive, my inner light is my fire.

On this 26th day of June, in this year of 2025,
I am very happy to say that I am still alive,
It's been seven years post, and I am living my life,
And I get to say that.......... with a great big smile.

The time has come to finish these writes,
Thanks for reading about my life,
It's been a challenge, but I'll always survive,
And don't you forget, to survive.....you have to fight.

Now it's seven years today, and I still defy the grave,
Mr. Reaper's gone away, it's a game he couldn't play,
And I am very happy to say that I am still alive today,
And I did it all my own way, so hip-hip-hooray!

While others may think of it as the brink, I prefer to call it the outlook,
And while I don't know what's ahead, I am willing to take a guess.

...................that it's going to be .....so Goddamn......
........So Goddamn................................Beautiful................

26 June, 2025

I Still Ain't Dead Yet

"Hey there, how are you going? Do you remember me?"
I am the guy, they said was dying, now here I am on my feet,
It hasn't been easy, it's been a challenge, but I always had belief,
So, while you might trying, I'll be doing..........I am the creator of me.

It was almost a decade ago, in a white hospital room,
That is when I was told, that my kidneys would be dead soon,
But little did they know, nor had they met me yet,
And as I foretold in the writes before this.......I still ain't dead yet!

"Hey, Troy, don't you know that you're going to die?"
"In fact, we're all amazed that you're still alive,"
"You see, you're down to just 1% of kidney functionality,"
"Hey, Troy, are you okay? Are you finding it hard to breathe?"

"Nah, Mate, I'm alright — you're talking to the wrong man,"
"I've heard the odds before and I've been burning through your plan,"
"You see, I came into this world already swinging at the dark,"
"So go ahead and write me off — I'll start again from scratch."

I push myself so much harder, so I can be stronger than the day before,
I hide my fear inside of laughter, my weakness is to be ignored,
And my Demons I will smother, I don't need any of them anymore,
And now I push myself so much harder, I am prepared for this war.

My body kept its word, it held the line,
The doctors read the numbers and went quiet for a time,
I'm doing things my way, unconventional and free,
And that is more than alright, I live, I fight, I breathe.

It was almost a decade ago, in a white hospital room
That is when I was told, that my kidneys would be dead soon
But little did they know, nor had they met me yet
And as I foretold in the writes before this........I still ain't dead yet!

I've tried to do this right, and I have done it all with utmost respect
For my Donor's life, and all the family that he has left
I do it with a smile, even though I am totally bathed in sweat
And just in case you didn't notice this............I still ain't dead yet!

5 April, 2026

181

Epilogue

Fifty-Six

It's been seven or eight months now,
Since I completed this series of writes,
And fifty-six is coming around soon,
So, I thought I'd revisit them again tonight.

From the very first incarnation of 'Have You Met Me Yet?'
There's been some tears, pain and frustration....and times when I've felt less,
But I found my inner Beast, the one that gave me the respect,
To understand myself, and to do things differently from the rest.

And now here we go, here we go, here we go again,
And now here we go, here we go again,
You know the one. You know the song,
....Have you met me yet?

"Hey, Troy. Don't you know that you're going to die?"
"In fact, we're all amazed that you're still alive,"
"You see, you're down to just 1% of kidney functionality,"
"Hey, Troy. Are you okay? Are you finding it hard to breathe?"

"Nah, Mate. I'm alright. I've got lots of fight left,"
"You tell me that I'm dying, but have you met me yet?"
"You see, there's something about me that you don't know,"
"I've been a fighter from birth, and I can still take all of these blows."

And then there was 'Nail Gun', the one about my kidney biopsy,
And the nurse who held my hand, even though it wasn't her responsibility,
I was still just trying to understand what the fuck was happening to me,
At first, there was so much fragility, but then I found my inner Beast,
Then I finally found out that there was so much more to this existence that is me.

That's when I decided to kill me weak, bruises fade with time,
My scars are the tattoos that you see, well, the ones on the outside,
They put a mountain in front of me, and that's when I started to climb,
You see, I can fall on my knees, but I will always rise.

And I always had my backup, my wonderful daughter, Kyra-Lee,
It's because of her that I stand up I am stronger than this damn disease,
And when I dug deep inside, that's when I released my inner Beast,
'Cause there's only one person that can save my life......and that is me.

So, I doubled down and then tripled down, I just put in the work,
In this life, there's no days off for me, no ceilings that I can't burst,
If pain was an excuse, I'd stay on my knees, but I know my own worth,
It's not my time to leave this life, even though sometimes it fucking hurts.

Hey, ho, here we go, here we go again,
It's that chorus that we all the know,
The one that never seems to end.....

"Hey, Troy. Don't you know that you're going to die?"
"In fact, we're all amazed that you're still alive,"
"You see, you're down to just 1% of kidney functionality,"
"Hey, Troy. Are you okay? Are you finding it hard to breathe?"

"Nah, Mate. I'm alright. I've got lots of fight left,"
"You tell me that I'm dying, but have you met me yet?"
"You see, there's something about me that you don't know,"
"I've been a fighter from birth, and I can still take all of these blows."

In the garden of adversity, that's where I will always thrive,
You can't put the hurt on me, I've lived it my entire life,
And now I've won the lottery, and for this I will always fight,
Because in the garden of adversity, I have learned to survive.

It's been seven or eight months now,
Since I completed this series of writes,
And fifty-six is coming around soon,
So, I thought I'd revisit them again tonight.

From the very first incarnation of 'Have You Met Me Yet?'
There's been some tears, pain and frustration....and times when I've felt less,
But I found my inner Beast, the one that gave me the respect,
To understand myself, and to do things differently from the rest.

So, now here we are, with the words on the page, will they even be read,
This took all of my heart, and a shitload of pain, but it all had to be said,
Some might ask, what happens from here, where will you go to next?
Well, as I've said, fifty-six is coming up, and my focus is purely on strength.

And now I am gyming every single day, even on days that I'm supposed to rest,
I put every ounce of my sweat into my pain, and I just can't relent,
I can be there for up to four hours a day, and Mr Reaper still hasn't caught me yet,
And now that fifty-six is coming around, I have to be better than the best.

You may of thought I was going hard before, but I'm just getting into my groove,
I've never needed affirmation before, and I can be my own muse,
It's like that chorus that never seems to end,
You know the one....."Have You Met Me Yet?"
And oh, hey, ho, here we go, here we go again,
It's that chorus that we all know, the one that never seems to end.

"Hey, Troy. Don't you know that you're going to die?"
"In fact, we're all amazed that you're still alive,"
"You see, you're down to just 1% of kidney functionality,"
"Hey, Troy. Are you okay? Are you finding it hard to breathe?"

"Nah, Mate. I'm alright. I've got lots of fight left,"
"You tell me that I'm dying, but have you met me yet?"
"You see, there's something about me that you don't know,"
"I've been a fighter from birth, and I can still take all of these blows."

You can be the victim or the victor, the choice is always yours,
You can break the system, you can use your voice,
Maybe they won't listen, and your words will just fall into the void,
But no one will ever hear them if you're afraid to make the choice,
So, I made all my own decisions, I had to become the God of Troy,
Because I'll never be the victim in this Goddamn war.

And now I'm getting older, and fifty-six is just around the corner,
But that's only in Earthly years, but body is a decade younger,
It's all about finding my strength, even on days when it feels much harder,
I don't care about pride or sin, the hard days just make me tougher.

And now it's finally time to put this series of writes to bed,
Thanks for reading all these pages, my unmet friends,
And when it comes time, and they question my strength,
I'll simply look back at them and say, "Have you met me yet?"

26 January, 2026

Troy Waz Here

And when the curtains finally close, for the very last time,
Just remember, I never lost hope, I fought so hard to stay alive,
I'd worked to extend the end of my rope, year after year after year,
And graffitied down the end of the road, in spray paint, is, 'Troy Waz Here.'

Yeah, I've lived, and I've fought the good fight,
But everything eventually comes to an end,
And I hope my daughter sees me in the stars tonight,
And remembers that love doesn't ever really end,

I really hope she knows she was my sun and sign,
And she's got so much of her life to live yet,
I really wish for her such a beautiful life,
And remembers about health, happiness and rest.

So, by now, you've read all these writes,
You get the story of, 'Have You Met Me Yet?'
I really don't love leaving, but I know this fight,
I hope I've shown my daughter how to represent.

HAVE YOU MET ME YET?

Just because it's the end of my life, she's got so much left,
And I hope if she's ever in strife, she mutters the words,
....."Have You Met Me Yet?".........

I've tried to be her example of how to tackle the tough times,
And when things were doubtful, I would always just smile,
And maybe she might mutter, or maybe she might shout,
Those five words she's heard, "Have You Met Me Yet?"

The reason that I wrote all this was just to leave something behind,
I just wanted to show my kid that, in a way, her Dad's still alive,
Show her that she can take her chances, after all, it's her turn next,
I just wish I were still here and able to see her words transferred to text.

But if she's missing me, she's got this book,
For a stroll down memory lane, or just a quick look,
And I hope my words will comfort her in future years,
And somewhere down the end of the road, if you look, you'll still see,
In spray paint on the wall, 'Troy Waz Here.'
..............'Troy Waz Here'.................

31 March, 2026

191

Thank You!

Thank you for reading all of this book. The following pages are the original version of "Have You Met Me Yet?" in song form. This is where it all began.

Have You Met Me Yet?

It was eight years ago, on the thirteenth day of June,
Doctors were surrounding me in a hospital room,
They all look at my chart as they shake their heads,
They're thinking to themselves, how is this guy not dead.

CHORUS

"Hey, Troy, don't you know that you're going to die?"
"In fact, we're all amazed that you're still alive,"
"You see, you're down to just 1% of kidney functionality,"
"Hey, Troy, are you okay? Are you finding it hard to breathe?"

"Nah, Mate, I'm alright, I've got lots of fight left,"
"You tell me that I'm dying, but have you met me yet?"
"You see, there's something about me that you don't know,"
"I've been a fighter from birth, I can take the blows."

I went to a doctor for a simple health check,
"Hey, Troy, while you're here, let's do some blood tests,"
"Are your kidneys okay? Are they working alright?'
"As far as I'm aware, doctor, my kidneys are doing fine,"
"Okay then, take these pills, your blood pressure's kinda high,"
"We should have all your results on Wednesday around five."

"Oh, it seems I may have prescribed you some of the wrong meds,"
"Your kidneys are now dying, in fact, they're almost dead,"
"You need to go to the hospital, there's not much time left,"
But I couldn't go, I had my daughter, it was our weekend.

REPEAT CHORUS

BRIDGE

We've got a drug for this, a drug for that, and everything in between,
Here you go, just swallow them down, and then take some more at three,
Now I'm medicated, and everything feels so slow,
Before I was asymptomatic, but now I'm in the throes,
I've mastered the old man shuffle, left, right, left, right, left,
But if I were going any slower, I'd be going in reverse instead.

"Hey, Troy, are you okay? Are you finding it hard to breathe?"
"If you are, we can help you; we've got all the pills you need,"
"Well, we don't want to worry you, but we've just got your results,"
"And we're very sad to say that we really don't like your odds."

"Well, call me a fool to believe in myself, I don't need your fucking help,"
"Here you are casting your shadows of doubt, but I will never doubt myself,"
"You don't even know me. I've got lots of fight left,"
"You tell me that I'm dying, but have you met me yet?"

REPEAT BRIDGE

REPEAT CHORUS

"Prepare for constipation, loss of urination, and constant irritation,"
"There's going to be frustration, risk of inflammation, as your system breaks down,"
"Immunosuppression, risk of rejection, it's just how it's all turned out,"
"But we're here to listen, if you wish it, until your last breath falls out."

It's a dance between two strangers, in such a primal way,
This cowardly disease, that thought a man like me could break,
It put me on my knees, but I knew I would rise again,
But here I am, you see, I'm standing here today.

REPEAT BRIDGE

Now the drugs aren't working anymore, and I'm dressed all in purple,
They're cutting me open again today, we're just waiting for the surgeons,
Unfortunately, it's not a one-off thing; I've lost count of all my procedures,
But I will tell you one thing I know, I won't be attending my own funeral.

REPEAT BRIDGE

REPEAT CHORUS

Counting all the doctors, 1, 2, 3, standing around a hospital room, all looking at me,
"We've got your new results, and they're not pretty. Creatinine is high, eGFR is dipping,"
"We've got you on the transplant list, cross your fingers and hope for the best,"
"It might be time to finalise things, write a will, and all the rest."

REPEAT CHORUS

It was six years ago, on the twenty-sixth day of June,
I was in the shower that morning, and my phone wasn't in the room,
I didn't hear the phone ring, I didn't see the missed call,
5 minutes later, there was a banging at my front door,
It was my brother, he said: "They've got a kidney for you!"
I had to get to the city, and I had to get there soon.

As I'm sure you can guess, I've made it to today,
But it hasn't been easy; I've had to sculpt a new me,
I've had to make changes, and I've made my mistakes,
But at least I'm alive today, so that I can make them again.

REPEAT BRIDGE

REPEAT CHORUS

"You tell me that I'm dying, but I've got lots of fight left,"
"After all, how would you know, have you met me yet?"

11 August, 2024

Foreword

Keep your eyes out for the upcoming new book! Here's a little tease of what you can expect.

DON'T BUY THIS!

Don't Buy This!

I arrive with purpose, in a non-traditional way,
I come full service, and you don't even have to pay,
Trust me, it's really worth it, just listen to what I have to say,
This is going to be perfect, so read these words today.

Don't buy this! It's all a fucking crook,
Don't buy this! You don't want to buy this book,
Don't buy this! You'll never put it down,
Don't buy this! Keep it safe where it can't be found,
Don't buy this! Don't you dare even take a look,
Don't buy this! I'm sure you'll love this book.

This book is all rubbish, just throw it in the bin,
But you might just discover the words written within,
Maybe they might let you, release yourself to sin,
I never said this was the Bible, and I say this with a wink.

Don't buy this! It's written really bad,
Don't buy this! Because you won't get your money back,
Don't buy this! It will really make you sad,
Don't buy this! 'Cause you can't bring it back.

This book is full of mutters, ramblings from a crazy man,
This book is full of nothing, turn the pages, they're all blank,
This book might give you comfort in a way that isn't bad,
This book is really something, give it to me, I want it back.

Don't buy this! It's just a pile of shit,
Don't buy this! You'll only throw it in the bin,
Don't buy this! But I know you can't resist,
Don't buy this! Keep it forever to pass down to your kids.

This book is contradictory, it says don't, but I do,
This book is supplementary to the evening NEWS,
This book is quite supreme, it tells a new truth,
This book was written by me, written for someone like you.

5 April, 2026

Saturday Night Just Don't Do It For Me Anymore

Running around, going crazy, acting like stupid little kids,
Throwing punches, like stupid bitches, fuck, I'm sick of this shit,
It's time to grow up, leave the kids we were in '86,
It's been a long time since we were kicking back in the sticks.

We've got jobs now, we've got families, we've got responsibilities,
We've got health plans, we've got SUVs, and debt that's neck deep,
The cost of living, rising prices, waiting on the next interest rate increase,
Electricity's rising, the rental crisis, and still the planet's not clean.

I'm not interested in going to nightclubs and showing I.D. at the door,
And parties seem to take so much more effort than before,
I'd rather stay at home and have some beers and just watch some sport,
And now Saturday night just don't do it for me anymore.

Is this what it's like now, being an adult, in the 21st century,
I just want to lie down, close my eyes now, and just go to sleep,
When I wake now, will the world be proud of what I have achieved,
Or will I fall down, stay on the ground, or get up with some dignity.

I'm not interested in going to nightclubs and showing I.D. at the door,
And parties seem to take so much more effort than before,
I'd rather stay at home and have some beers and just watch some sport,
And now Saturday night just don't do it for me anymore.

Ten o'clock in the evening seems so much later, as I have aged,
Usually, you'll find me sleeping on the couch, well before eight,
I get up early in the morning, yeah, I've joined the gym brigade,
And I'll keep doing it, like an addict, always trying to reverse my age.

We've got jobs now, we've got families, we've got responsibilities,
We've got health plans, we've got SUVs, and debt that's neck deep,
The cost of living, rising prices, waiting on the next interest rate increase,
Electricity's rising, the rental crisis, and still the planet's not clean.

Now I'm more of a homebody, with my creature comforts, I've got all that I need,
Bar fridge is full of VB's, the vinyls pumping, as I'm watching cricket on TV,
Why do I need to go out at night time? It's not fun like it was before,
I get all that I need, delivered to my door,
..........And Saturday night just don't do it for me anymore.

14 January, 2026

Jacket Off

I feel my soul trying to separate itself from myself.
Just like taking a jacket off after a long night out.
I feel myself looking for a way with eyes blacked out,
And I just can't help myself, I can't help myself.

I've tried, I've tried, I've tried,
And I just can't help myself,
I've tried, I've tried, I've tried,
And I only blame myself,
I've tried, I've tried, I've tried,
And I am still trying,
I've tried, I've tried, I've tried,
And I just can't help myself,
I've tried, I've tried, I've tried,
...and I've tried.

You only...expose me,
You only...make me look weak,
You only...want to control me,
You only...want me to bleed.

I'm not your puppet on a string,
There ain't no button to make me sing,
I've been around this thing,
Time and time again,
I've been around this thing,
I've been inside your machine.

And now... the emptiness bleeds out of me until the floor is stained,
And now... everyone can finally see the beast that can't be chained,
And now...everyone knows the real me,
I am, I am, I am... finally the monster that your hand created me to be!

Look what you created,
From just a mere man,
Look what you then hated,
Made by your own hand.

I can't win, I can't win, I can only lose,
I can't win, I can't win, I can only burn, a slow-fusing wick,
I can't win, I can't win, I can only lose,
I can't win, I can't win, if I never learn how to break the script,
I can't win, I can't win, I can't win,
When will it finally be my turn to be more than the fuel for this thing?

I feel my soul trying to separate itself from myself,
Just like taking a jacket off after a long night out,
I feel myself looking for a way with eyes blacked out,
And I just can't help myself, I can't help myself.

The Devil has a place set for me at his table,
He's promised me my own special kind of crown,
But I'm still holding out for the Angel,
I'm still holding out for the Angel,
...before my breath runs out.

You only, you only, want to make me look weak,
You only, you only, ever want to expose me,
You only, you only, ever want to watch me bleed,
You only, you only, you only want to control me.

I've tried, I've tried, and I've tried again,
But I am now done with doing this thing,
I'm done, I'm done and won't ever begin,
Doing this thing with you again.

I ain't your puppet on a string,
I ain't your toy play thing,
I am over your everything,
I am over you and your ******* ****.

And I just can't help myself, I can't help myself,
I guess you'll always track me down,
And I just can't help myself, I can't help myself,
I feel you in my veins now,
And I just can't help myself, I can't help myself,
You're toxic for me...and I don't want anyone else.

6 December, 2026

Energiser Bunny With Home Brand Batteries

I'm the Energiser Bunny, but I've only got Home Brand batteries,
I might be running fast, just like someone is chasing me,
But that just doesn't last, it is a limited supply of energy,
So while I still have charge, you'll only see the best of me.

Lift that weight, and then lift that weight again,
Grinding for the spark I need,
Do the repetitions, until the sets become the only rhythm that I bleed,
Lift that weight, and then lift that weight again,
Legs, then chest, then the racing heart,
Trying to lap the circuit twice before the batteries fall apart.

Lift that weight, and then lift that weight again,
I can't forget my arms, then cardio will be next,
So I'll lift that weight, and then lift that weight again,
In between the sets, there is just no rest for me,
I'll take a couple of breaths, and then I'll return to speed.

I'm running once again, sometimes I do it breathlessly,
And well before I'm done, there's no differentiation between the sweat and me,
Yeah, I'm running fast, and I do it relentlessly,
I've got a circuit coming up, not once, but twice around for me.

I like to double up, I expect so much more from me,
I use it while it lasts, by the time I'm home, I'm collapsible me,
I'm the Energiser Bunny, but I've only got Home Brand batteries,
I make sure I'm at full charge before jumping into the driver's seat,
Programs are on the cards, I've got 4 and ½ hours of gymming for me,
And I lap it up, the hardness, the pain...is the strength I need.

Lift that weight, and then lift that weight again
Do the repetitions until they lead to sets
Lift that weight, and then lift that weight again
First, I'll do legs, and then move onto chest

Lift that weight, and then lift that weight again,
I can't forget my arms, then cardio will be next,
So I'll lift that weight, and then lift that weight again.

While I still have charge, you'll only see the best of me,
Running breathless and fast, because the 'collapsible me' is chasing me,
But the spark is dimming; it's a cheap and limited supply of energy,
I'm the Energiser Bunny, held together by these Home Brand batteries.

2 April, 2026

The Sheep People

There's flocks of sheep disguised as people bleating for a shepherd's hand,
While the masses trade their voices for a subservient place to stand,
The hurting are a statistic, and the Government's a ghost in the chair,
Where only the elite own the walls, and soon they'll be tax-stamping the air.

.You've gotta fire up this world,
Put a firecracker right under its arse,
It is time to be heard,
Before they fuck this world up.

We're just refusing to think for ourselves, now that AI is our new God,
We just ask our artificial assistant to deal with all our wants,
Where the hell is the resistance? They'll eventually replace us with bots,
But the sheep people keep on bleating, as long as the scraps are enough.

Don't you know that you are worth more, more than what you're told,
Every day there is a new dawn, make it yours to unfold,
Don't be one of the sheep people; you can pave your own way,

Now there seems to be no deep people; they have all been enslaved.
Whatever happened to just doing the right thing,
Can we blame it on NASA or alien spaceships?
Have we lost our decency? Have we simply lost our way,
We've forgotten our history; is the future already computer screen saved.

We could be relinquishing, while on our knees we pray,
This feeling of emptiness, this emotional break,
But we're not remembering the mistakes that we make,
The sheep people are bleating, but have nothing to say.

You've gotta fire up this world,
Put a firecracker right under its arse,
It is time to be heard,
Before they fuck this world up.

Are we even going to leave a footprint for our kids to follow,
Besides the famine and the wars and a world that's turned hollow?
Will they look back through their screens and never forgive what we did,
Having traded their green earth for this grey and broken grid?
We should have left a legacy that was much better than this.

But the sheep people are bleating, without having anything to say,
While the fat cats are laughing, smoking cigars and drinking champagne,
I'm worried this world is leading the last of the good people astray,
But the sheep people are bleating...hoping there's money to be made.

1 April, 2026

Ancestral Anxiety

I can see it in my mind, as I throw this bottle against the wall,
There's something not quite right, all my Demons are at war,
There's something just out of sight, I can feel it in my core,
Maybe it's just my ancestral anxiety, coming to the fore.

It's like a crash and a bang, the heavy toll of the trap,
The first strike that stings with the sound of a slap,
It's like the crack of a back that's been bent until it snaps,
When you're broken in two and fall through the gaps,
It's like the clap of a whack that strikes from behind your back,
Leaving me like a man in a foreign land, staring at the map,
Watching a world I once knew finally fade into black.

I don't know why I do these things,
Can I blame it on my Demons within,
Maybe I'm psycho, maybe I'm just sick,
And I don't know why I do these things.

I can hear the screams inside as my fist makes contact with the bricks,
There's a war going on in my mind, as the skin on my fist begins to split,
First I'm low, and then I'm high, as my blood paints a portrait of my regret,
There's no way that I can deny all these Demons that are fighting in my head.

I don't know why I do these things,
Is this ancestral anxiety coming through?
I don't know why there's blood on my fist,
And on these bricks, painted in a portrait so blue.

Is it just genetics, all the pain of the people before me,
I just don't get it. Is this a kind of ancestral anxiety,
Are these just excuses for the Demons inside of me,
Maybe I'm just Evil, and my Monsters, they lie to me.

It's like a crash and a bang,
The fist strike that sounds like a slap,
It's like the crack of a back,
When you're broken in two like that,
It's like the clap of a whack,
That you cop from behind your back,
I'm just like a man in a foreign land,
And I just do not understand.

Do blue eyes give you a mean streak, just like a cruel drunk,
But what if they are green, would that be change enough?
Nothing is as it seems when you get under the skin to the blood,
Is this ancestral anxiety, or am I just coming undone,
Is this ancestral anxiety, or am I just doing this all for fun...

20 March, 2026

Superheroes

Where have all the superheroes gone,
Are there anymore around these days?
Are the aliens ever going to come?
In their spaceships from outer space,
Will Jesus be risen once again,
So that we can all be saved,
Where have all the superheroes gone,
Maybe they're praying for better days.

Is reality even real anymore?
Or are we living in a different dimension?
Did something slip that created the fall?
Is AI the new religion?

I don't know what we're doing this for,
Have we given up science for science fiction?
What the hell are superheroes for?
If they lack the courage of their conviction.

When this Human race is at war, we're only burying the future in the mud,
But when they sell it as democracy, we trade our conscience for their blood,
I don't know about you, but I refuse to read from their hollowed-out scripts,
Where the truth is written in scriptures that have been rewritten in the pits;
Maybe it's a darkness I can't describe, a ghost I can't quite capture,
But I won't show you in pictures the horror of this final, manufactured chapter.

Where have all the superheroes gone,
Are there no more humans who have conviction?
Or are we just waiting on more?
...Hollywood Science Fiction...

25 March, 2026

I'll See You On The Other Side

When the night slays the day that was previously made,
And all the leaders have decimated the entire Human race,
I really hope they enjoy all the dollars they have made,
I really do hope that they feel worshipped and are praised.

Yeah, I say all of this with a very sarcastic taste,
Because sometimes I wonder...are we worthy of being saved?
Whilst the majority of us remain enslaved,
And now we have the new Gods that have been given new names,
But it's alright, we're all going to be saved,
We just won't realise that we're in invisible chains.

I'll see you on the other side, my friend,
When the movie is over, and the credits begin,
I'm hoping they're making a sequel to this,
So we can relive all of our greatest hits.

Because the kids of the future will never know a world they can't just swipe away,
Inheriting a digital ghost of the past while our future turns to grey,
It's all in cold emails instead of letters; the mercy of the machine is coming with speed,
Technology promised us a bridge, but it only built the division that we bleed,
Why can't we just reach out a hand and remember what a human community means?
Instead of scrolling past the wreckage... and the fact that I am now at severe risk of homelessness.

The first thing I did was write to the Prime Minister's Office,
And just in case he didn't answer, I wrote the QLD Premier,
I know in the scheme of things, I'm just a problem,
But I'm a problem that's not going anywhere.

So then I just do some more writing, to local politicians instead,
And hey, I got a call in, and now it's not just me and my head,
I have people advocating because they know my health is at risk,
But the problem is that there is no housing...and homelessness would lead to my death,
And there's no point in praying to a God that isn't even there,
I'm used to solving my own problems, hey, have you met me yet?

So I'm gonna be Batman instead of Robin, I have the starring role,
Like, have you met me yet? I'm always the one in control,
But just in case the housing doesn't come through...well...
Remember me in my writes...and the stories they tell...
Just in case I'm not here to tell you tonight...

1 April, 2026

www.ingramcontent.com/pod-product-compliance
Lightning Source LLC
Chambersburg PA
CBHW032232050726

47591CB00001B/366